# THE NORTHERN WORLD

Adapted from TO THE ENDS OF THE EARTH
by Irene M. Franck and David M. Brownstone

A Volume in the Trade and Travel Routes Series

## Facts On File

*New York • Oxford • Sydney*

**The Northern World**

| | | |
|---|---|---|
| Facts On File, Inc. | Facts On File Limited | Facts On File Pty Ltd |
| 460 Park Avenue South | Collins Street | Talavera & Khartoum Rds |
| New York NY 10016 | Oxford OX4 1XJ | North Ryde NSW 2113 |
| USA | United Kingdom | Australia |

**Library of Congress Cataloging-in-Publication Data**

The Northern world: adapted from To the ends of the earth by Irene M.
    Franck and David M. Brownstone.
        p.    cm. — (Trade and travel routes series)
    Bibliography: p.
    Includes index.
    Summary: A historical survey of the major trade and travel routes
across the North Atlantic, through Canada, and around the Arctic
Circle.
    ISBN 0-8160-1879-0
    1. Trade routes—Northern Hemisphere—History—Juvenile
literature.  2. Northern Hemisphere—Commerce—History  Juvenile
literature.  [1. Trade routes—Northern Hemisphere—History.]
    I. Franck, Irene M.  To the ends of the earth.  II. Series.
HE328.N67  1990
382'.09181'3—dc20                89-11701

British and Australian CIP data available on request from Facts On File.

Facts On File books are available at special discounts when purchased in bulk quantities for businesses, associations, institutions or sales promotion. Please contact the Special Sales Department of our New York office at 212/683-2244 (dial 800/322-8755 except in NY, AK or HI).

Jacket design by Catherine Hyman
Composition by Facts On File, Inc.
Manufactured by R. R. Donnelley & Sons
Printed in the United States of America

10 9 8 7 6 5 4 3 2 1

This book is printed on acid-free paper.

Franck, M. Irene & Brownstone,
M. David

The Northern World

| DATE DUE | | | |
|---|---|---|---|
| DEC 1 9 2012 | | | |
| | | | |
| | | | |
| | | | |
| | | | |
| | | | |
| | | | |
| | | | |
| | | | |
| | | | |
| | | | |

# CONTENTS

# LIST OF MAPS

# PREFACE

*The Northern World* is one volume in the Trade and Travel Routes series. The series itself is based on our earlier work, *To the Ends of the Earth*, published by Facts On File, Inc. in 1984. This adaptation of the work for young readers has been prepared by Facts On File; many new illustrations have also been added.

Several publishers gave permission to reprint selections from their works. In this volume, the excerpt on p. 34 is quoted from *The Vinland Sagas: the Norse Discovery of America*, translated by Magnus Magnusson and Hermann Pálsson, copyright © Magnus Magnusson and Hermann Pálsson 1965. The maps, drawn from *To the Ends of the Earth*, are by Dale Adams.

*Irene M. Franck*
*David M. Brownstone*

# INTRODUCTION

## What Is a Trade Route?

In a world without airplanes, engine-powered ships, trucks, or even paved roads, how did people journey from one place to another? How did products that were found only in a very small part of the world eventually find their way across the continents? For almost five thousand years, people have been bringing products from one part of the world to another using trade routes. Traders from Europe, Asia, and Africa carried furs, spices, silks, pottery, knives, stone utensils, jewels, and a host of other commodities, exchanging the products found in one area for the products found in another.

When trading first began, there were no real roads. Local traders might follow trails or cross steep mountain passes in their treks from one village to another. With the passage of time, tracks might be widened and eventually paved. But the new paved roads tended to follow the old trade routes, establishing these routes as important links of communication between different cultures.

As technology advanced, sea-lanes became vital trade routes between the various continents, and made possible trade with North America, South America, and Australia. Many of the highways and seaways that have been used predominantly for trade throughout history have shaped its course of events because of the many ways in which the routes have been used.

## Why Study Trade Routes?

Studying the trade routes is one way of learning about the history of the world. As we look at the trade routes of Europe, for example, we can see how the nations of that continent have changed throughout the centuries: we learn how Scandinavian Vikings came to sail south and west to settle in France and Britain; we can appreciate how present-day Hungary was originally settled by a wandering tribe from the Ural Mountains, etc. In a similar way, by looking at the trade routes of Africa, we can trace the history of the slave trade and learn about the European colonization of Africa in the 18th and 19th centuries.

In addition, studying the trade routes helps us better understand the origin of many of the institutions and services with which we are familiar today. Postal systems, tolls, guidebooks, roadside restaurants and hotels all came into being, either directly or indirectly, because of trade routes. Studying the trade routes will help you to understand how they emerged.

## How to Use This Book

This book is organized in chapters. Each chapter is devoted to the history of one trade route, or in some cases, where the particular trade route has an especially long and eventful past, to a particular era in a trade route's history. Therefore, you can simply read about one trade route that particularly interests you or, alternatively, read about all the trade routes in a given area. At the end of each chapter, you will find a list of books for further reading, which will assist you in locating additional sourcebooks should you need them to support report research or classroom work. If you are using these books as references for a particular history course, check the index of each to find the subject or person you need to know more about. The list of maps at the front of this book will direct you to all maps contained herein, and thereby help you to locate each trade route on the face of the earth.

Studying trade routes can be a fascinating way of learning about world history—and of understanding more about our lives today. We hope you enjoy all the volumes in the TRADE AND TRAVEL ROUTES series.

# 1

# THE WESTERN SEAWAYS AND THE TIN ROUTES

The Western Seaways are a series of sea lanes around the coast of Europe. They start at the Strait of Gibraltar, off the coast of Spain. Then they work their way north, past the British Isles, up past Scandinavia, all the way to Finland and the Soviet Union.

These sea routes go back to ancient times, many thousands of years B.C. In those times, the area that we now call "Europe" was very different from the way it is today. Today, we know Europe as a group of nations—France, Spain, Italy, West Germany, etc. The people who live in these nations are citizens of a country—France, Spain, or some other nation. The people also consider themselves part of the continent of Europe, sharing some of their history and culture with other Europeans.

But in very ancient times, the European continent was not divided up into individual countries. People lived in small villages, which were isolated from other villages by a day or two's worth of travel. Traders and other travelers might have a picture of the world that went past the next village—but even they could not picture the geography of a whole continent the way we can today.

Of course, under these conditions, people did not think of themselves as "Europeans." They thought of themselves as members of their local village.

Gradually, people began to explore beyond their own territories and travel to other villages. By sea and by land, those in one village went in search of other people and places, near and far. Sometimes

1

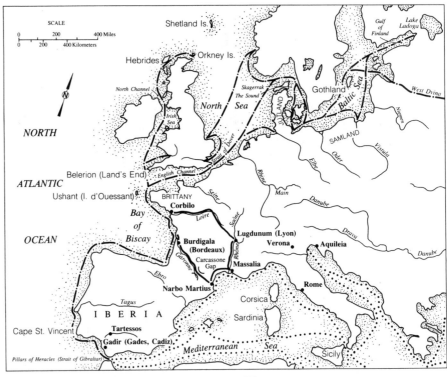

*The Western Seaways in Pre-Roman Times*

—·—·—·— Western Seaways          · · · · · · · Main Connecting Routes

——————— Tin Routes

they were forced to travel because of drought and famine. Other times they traveled to trade their goods—such as furs, tools, and ornaments—for goods which were not available in their own region.

Over the centuries, people began to group together in larger numbers to form cities, and to form larger political units. Some countries progressed more quickly than others and created empires which conquered peoples in other lands. The map of Europe was continually changing. Also changing were Europe's languages, and its peoples. Many of the people living in Europe today have ancestors who originally came from a different part of the world.

The story of the Western Seaways and the Tin Routes is the story of the development of Europe. Over the centuries, people in Europe were motivated to travel and explore. Sometimes they simply wanted to trade with other peoples. Sometimes they wanted to conquer other nations, or to invade and settle there. Whatever their motivations, the process of trade, travel, and exploration continued, until people realized the true extent and size of the European continent. The Western Seaways and the Tin Routes played an important part in establishing for people just how big Europe was.

## Geography of the Western Seaways

There are two basic routes of the Western Seaways. Both routes begin in Gibraltar and run up along the Atlantic coast. Both go to the area of France known as Brittany, and to the English Channel—the narrow strip of water that separates England from France.

One branch goes from the tip of Brittany into the Irish Sea, through the narrow North Channel between Ireland and Scotland. It passes the Western Isles of Scotland and joins the North Atlantic Route which later explorers used to travel to America.

The other branch of the Western Seaways passes through the English Channel and through the Strait of Dover, where there are famous white cliffs made of chalk. This second branch links up with some of the great rivers of northern Europe: the Seine in France, the Thames in England, and the Rhine in the Netherlands and West Germany. This branch then goes into the North Sea, around Denmark, past Sweden, and into the Baltic Sea. It connects with some rivers of the Soviet Union and Poland as it passes into the Gulf of Finland, where it links up with more Russian rivers.

You can see how the Seaways linked different areas of northern Europe. Traders and travelers could go by river through their own countries, and sail onto the Western Seaways to connect with other countries.

**Difficult Routes.**   The Western Seaways were attractive to sailors because they had many sheltered harbors. Sailors could pull into a harbor and know that they were safe from storms while they anchored their ship for the night.

However, because the Seaways ran so close to the coast, they passed many *capes* and *peninsulas*, pieces of land jutting out into the water. There were often rocky areas, dangerous for sailing. Often, travelers had to *portage*, to carry or drag their goods and their boats across the land, until they could get back to the sea.

## Early Times

**The Archaeologist Detectives.**   When we study ancient times, we often have great difficulty in finding written records. Many ancient peoples had no written language. Even if they did, many of their records are now lost.

*Archaeologists* are scientists who study the past through its *artifacts*, objects that have lasted for thousands of years while buried in the ground or crumbling into ruins. They have found ways of figuring out some things about the history of ancient peoples, even those who did not keep records.

Archaeologists have found that the ancient peoples of Europe traveled to visit one another, probably to trade. They have found objects in grave sites or ancient garbage heaps that originally came from places tens or even hundreds of miles away. Based on these ancient objects, archaeologists have deduced that people traveled many hundreds of miles across the open water.

***Changes in Geography.*** We also know that the Western Seaways could not have been used before 5500 B.C., for they did not exist at that time. One of the stages in the history of the Earth is called the *Ice Age*. This was a period when the climate of the Earth was freezing. Glaciers moving across the land helped to shape the valleys and mountains that we know today. Glaciers also formed lakes and other features of the landscape.

During the Ice Age, the British Isles were still connected to Europe. Then, after the glaciers receded, the British Isles began to subside. Eventually the waters of the Atlantic rushed in and flowed over the areas that the Strait of Dover and the North Sea occupy today to create new areas of sea.

Before this happened, people were able to live in these areas, since they were still land. When the seas took their places, people began crossing the seas instead. By 3500 B.C., when the seas reached the level they have today, people began making contact across the waters.

How do we know this? Archaeologists have found tools dating from that period in southern France, Cornwall (a region in England), northeast Ireland, the Isle of Man (an island in the Irish Sea), and the Western Isles of Scotland. All the tools they have found are similar, which suggests that people were trading and sharing information with each other.

These peoples probably used boats made from animal skins sewn on frames and sealed with pitch (sticky sap from trees). They also used *dugouts*—canoes *dug out* of logs. We know about the dugouts because some of them have been found in Danish peat bogs, where they have lasted for thousands of years. Imagine crossing a stormy sea in a tiny boat, or riding along a rocky coast in a dugout!

Archaeologists have also found evidence that people along the eastern branch of the Western Seaways were sharing their culture with people in the west. They have found stone axes that they know were made in Central Europe—but the axes were discovered on the Scandinavian coast, and in Britain.

Other practices that spread along the Western Seaways included farming and taming animals. This seems to have spread from northern Europe into the British Isles almost 4,000 years ago, in about 2000 B.C.

## THE STONE AGE

Historians of ancient people have divided this early period into different sections, or *ages*. First came the *Stone Age*, when people learned how to make things out of stone. If you had only been able to use wood or straw before, imagine how important stone would be.

During this period, people built huge communal graveyards marked by giant stones, called *megaliths*. Stonehenge, in England, is an example of a megalithic site, where gigantic stones stand around in a circle.

Archaeologists and historians do not know exactly how these stones were used or what significance they had. We only know very little about the ancient religions of these times. We do know,

Great megaliths, like Stonehenge in Britain, were erected by people along the Western Seaways 3,500 to 4,000 years ago. (From James Henry Breasted, *Ancient Times: A History of the Early World...*, 1914)

however, that people during this time must have been traveling around by sea, for such megalithic circles appear in Brittany, which is in northern France, in England, and in Scotland.

***The Discovery of Copper.*** In about 2000 B.C., people of Atlantic Europe learned how to work with metal. (People in Africa and other parts of the world had learned this skill much earlier.) The people who lived around the Danube River in Central Europe had found out how to work with copper.

These people were known as the Bell-Beaker Folk, because they made beautiful pottery beakers (pitchers) shaped like bells. They traveled through much of Western Europe, using their copperworking skills where they could.

Some of the Bell-Beaker Folk came to be known as the *Celts*. This important group was to become the ancestor of many European cultures. They probably brought their knowledge of copperworking across the sea to the British Isles in about 1800 B.C.

## THE BRONZE AGE

Then came a very important discovery, so important that historians have used it to name the next great era—the Bronze Age. People learned that by mixing copper with tin, they could make a much harder metal, called *bronze*.

The only problem was, tin was hard to find. However, there are sources of tin in Cornwall, Brittany, and Spain. The attempts to find and develop these sources were the inspiration for much travel along the Western Seaways during this period.

At first, Western Europeans didn't need very much tin. They probably got all the bronze they wanted from traveling bronze-smiths, who made daggers and axes.

Many of these artifacts came from Ireland, which has little or no tin of its own. Yet archaeologists have found many old bronzeworking sites around the place that is now the city of Belfast. Clearly, traders were carrying tin from other places up to Ireland, where there were many skilled workers to make it into useful objects. Archaeologists have also found old stoneworking sites in this area, so perhaps Ireland had a tradition of supplying its neighbors with high-quality products.

In 1500 B.C., then, there seems to have been a sea route in use for trade between the British Isles and Europe, crossing the English

Channel and the North Sea. European tin went to Ireland, and fine Irish metalwork went to Europe.

As the centuries continued, trade in general continued to grow. The archaeologist detectives found one important clue: a ship that sank off the coast of Spain. This shipwreck left new evidence of trade. It was carrying jewelry from the British Isles, and also from Sicily, the island just south of Italy.

Archaeologists have found other examples of items from faraway places. In the Outer Hebrides Islands north of Scotland, for example, they have found glass from the Mediterranean, bronzework from Europe, and amber (a gold-colored, fossilized resin used in jewelry) from the Baltic. This leads them to imagine that there was widespread trade in the early years.

However, everything that we know about these early times is really guesswork. We know almost nothing directly about the early peoples who traveled the Western Seaways.

## MEDITERRANEANS AND CELTS

In this same early period—around 2000 B.C.—traders from the eastern Mediterranean were moving west, toward Spain. They were also looking for new metal sources.

**Cretans.** The first to sail west and begin to develop the Western Seaways route were probably sailors from Crete. Crete is an island that today is part of Greece. In those days, it was a separate nation with its own culture and political system.

As you might expect of people who lived on an island, the Cretans were good sailors. They were interested in trading with the other peoples whom they could reach by sea. However, their tiny island was racked with earthquakes and invasions, which disrupted their traveling and trading.

**Greeks.** From 2500 B.C. onward, the Greeks began developing a culture that is in many ways the ancestor of Western civilization today. Their ideas about philosophy, art, and democracy form the basis of many modern-day Western cultures, while their studies and advances in anatomy, astronomy, and physics began the Western study of science as we know it.

The Greeks were also good sailors, and they also sailed west to Spain. In the middle of the seventh century B.C., they reached

Tartessos, the metal-rich region above what is today the Spanish city of Seville. This region had large amounts of copper, gold, silver, and, most importantly, tin. So the Greeks eagerly—and profitably— traded their goods for raw metal ingots (an ingot is a lump of metal).

***Phoenicians.*** The ancient Phoenicians were originally based in the area that today is the coast of Lebanon. They later established outposts in northern Africa, including the city of Carthage, which was located in present-day Tunisia. The Phoenicians eventually lost control of their homeland, but kept control of Carthage, so they became known as the Carthaginians.

The Phoenicians were famous sailors in their time. They were highly skilled navigators who had acquired much knowledge about the world around them. They also sailed north and west to Spain, where they founded a city called Gadir (today it's called Cadiz). They also founded a place called Algeciras just a few miles beyond the Strait of Gibraltar.

The Strait of Gibraltar separates Europe from Africa. It is a narrow ocean passage between rocky shores, and it is only nine miles wide. By about 530 B.C., the Phoenicians were strong enough to close the strait to all but Phoenician ships. The Phoenicians clearly wanted to be the only traders in the region. They destroyed the rival Greek city of Tartessos, to get rid of their competition.

With war galleys like this one from the sixth century B.C., Phoenicians sailed from the Mediterranean into the Western Seaways, and closed the Strait of Gibraltar behind them. (By Manning de V. Lee, in Rupert Sargent Holland, *Historic Ships*, 1926)

The Phoenicians may not have stayed only in Spain. Some Greek writers say that they went up the Coast to Brittany to buy tin. However, archaeologists have not been able to find any evidence of this. Perhaps Celtic traders brought tin south to trade with the Phoenicians. The Phoenicians needed tin from somewhere, for Spanish sources were running out.

***Secrets of the Phoenicians.*** The Phoenicians kept no written records, despite their advanced writing system, because they were afraid that their rivals would find out their secrets.

The Phoenicians were so worried about other people finding out what they knew that they actively told lies about trade routes and navigation. They made up stories filled with mistakes, so that others could not find the routes that the Phoenicians had found. They also told fantastic tales of monsters. However, they might honestly have believed their own horror stories. Perhaps their "sea monsters" were the whales that could then be found off the coast of Spain.

In any case, the Phoenicians went to great lengths to keep their secrets. Once, a Roman ship tried to follow a Phoenician ship, to learn its route. When the Phoenician captain saw this, he wrecked his own ship, so that the Roman ship would follow and be wrecked, too.

The Phoenicians may have sailed all the way north on the Western Seaways. Archaeologists have found some evidence of this: there are some Carthaginian coins on the Azores Islands, 900 miles out into the Atlantic. If the Phoenicians/Carthaginians did get this far, no other people at the time knew about it, for there are no written records of the journey.

***Celts.*** At the same time, the Celts were moving across Europe. This people became the ancestors of many modern European groups today, particularly the Scottish and the Irish. At this early time, they settled in the areas that today are France, Germany, Spain, and Portugal. By 100 B.C., they controlled much of the Atlantic coastline of France, Spain, and Portugal.

The Celts were good sailors, and they traveled all along the Atlantic seaboard. They went along the coast of Spain and France, around the tips of Brittany (in France) and Cornwall (in Britain), and into the Irish Sea. They used this route to unite all the different Celts in Europe. They also used it to trade tin with the Greeks and other merchants.

The next big changes in trading patterns happened during the period of the Roman Empire. The Romans were rulers of a huge empire that stretched across Europe and Asia, governing many peoples in many lands.

***The History of the Roman Empire.*** Rome began as a small city in the area that today is the modern country of Italy. But the people of Rome began to conquer first neighboring cities, then the whole territory of Italy, then outlying areas. Eventually they ruled in the areas that today are Greece, France, Britain, Spain, and Portugal, as well as parts of Germany, Turkey, and other Asian countries.

The Roman Empire helped to shape the language and culture of Europe as we know it today. When the Romans conquered a native people, they made the Roman language of Latin the official language. This language is at the root of the modern languages of French, Spanish, Italian, and Portuguese.

The Roman Empire also affected Europe's religion. At the end of the empire's rule, it adopted Christianity as its official religion. The Roman version of Christianity was the ancestor of today's Catholic Church, whose Pope, or leader, still leads the Church from Rome. Today, many of the territories that were under Roman rule—France, Spain, Portugal, Italy, and parts of Germany—still have a large proportion of Catholics in the population.

***Romans on Land and Sea.*** When the Romans conquered an area, they brought in soldiers to enforce their rule. They also brought in political officials to govern. These people needed roads to travel between Rome and the conquered territories. Traders, merchants, and messengers also needed roads to connect Rome to its colonies.

The Romans learned how to build excellent roads, many of which are the basis for modern highways of today. But they were landlubbers, preferring not to travel by sea. Therefore, when they gained power over most of Europe, they drastically affected the way trading was done. When they conquered Iberia (the region that today is Spain and Portugal), they discovered new sources of tin in Spain. After this, they needed less northern tin, and did not have to trade with the Celts.

The Romans and the Celts were enemies. In 56 B.C., the famous Roman leader, Julius Caesar, conquered the Celtic peoples of Brittany. He destroyed their fleet of wooden ships with leather sails—the ships that they had used to carry tin from Cornwall down to Spain.

The great days of the tin routes were over. For many centuries after the Romans conquered most of Europe's Atlantic coast, trade and travel was concentrated around land routes rather than sea routes.

## MIGRATIONS

Although they were not much used for trade and travel, the Western Seaways were used for *migrations*. A migration is when a people leaves its homeland in search of another home. Roman domination caused many people to leave the conquered lands in search of new places to live.

One of the first such migrations was that of the Celts. When Julius Caesar conquered Gaul (modern France) and Brittany, many Celts fled across the English Channel to Cornwall. Then the Romans conquered Britain in 43 A.D.

Thus, at this time, the people who lived in southern Britain faced a double invasion—one by the Celts and one by the Romans. They tried to migrate farther north. But they were blocked by another people, the Brigantes, who held the middle area of England, known as the Midlands.

So the refugees took the old sea routes northward. They settled first in the Western Isles of Scotland. They built their amazing *brochs*—huge stone towers. They also began working with iron, at the beginning of the next major age—the Iron Age. Iron was an even stronger and more durable metal than bronze.

These peoples soon traveled by land and sea to other parts of the region, including the Outer Hebrides, the Orkneys, the Shetlands, and the Scottish Highlands. There they merged with the other peoples who had settled in these regions over the previous centuries.

Little trade was carried on amongst these peoples, and their lives still focused on the Seaways. They depended upon fishing and whaling, and they also needed boats to travel around the islands of their own region. They used boats known as *curraghs* and *coracles*. Curraghs had frames made out of wicker—thin strips of wood—with animal skins sewn over the frame.

Moving from island to island along the Western Seaways, Celts often used small *coracles*, like this one, made of hide sewn together over a wicker framework. (Deutsches Museum, Munich)

### The Romans Leave Britain.

In around 400 A.D., the Romans finally left Britain. Then the Western Seaways became important once again—for new peoples used it to invade this land.

The Angles and the Saxons from Germany and the Jutes from Jutland (modern Denmark) sailed across the North Sea. They entered Britain from the east, and settled most of southern, central, and northeastern England. The people who had been living in those lands were pushed into the western lands bordering the Irish Sea, especially Wales and Cornwall.

## THE MISSIONARY ROUTES

The next people to use the Western Seaways were missionaries. Missionaries travel to distant lands to try to convert people to their religion. In the fifth century, many Christian missionaries went to Cornwall, Wales, and elsewhere in the British Isles.

### The History of Early Christianity.

To understand the story of the missionaries on the Western Seaways, we have to look at the history of Christianity. The religion of Christianity began with the life of Jesus, whose followers considered him the son of God. Therefore they called him Christ, or God.

Jesus lived in Palestine, a land in the Middle East which today is the country of Israel. In those days, it was a colony held by the

Romans. After Jesus' death, his followers began to preach their new religion throughout the Roman Empire.

At first, this new religion was mocked and ignored. Jesus had been born into the Jewish religion, which was a minority religion. The Romans did not accept Christianity since they had their own religion.

Gradually, however, the new religion of Christianity spread throughout the Roman Empire. In the fourth century A.D., the Roman Emperor Constantine converted to Christianity, and made it the official religion of the Roman Empire. As we have seen, this was a major turning-point that had a great impact on the culture and religion of Europe for many centuries, even down to our own day.

In the fifth century A.D., the Roman Empire began to decline. Waves of peoples from the East moved into Europe. The Romans could not incorporate these new people into their empire. When they tried to conquer the immigrants, the Romans had to take troops out of the other colonies they held.

The Romans did not have enough soldiers to keep control of all their territories. Gradually, the Roman Empire lost its power over Europe, and territories became independent once again. Even while the Roman Empire fell, however, the influence of Christianity continued to grow.

***Christianity in Britain.*** Naturally, many people migrated during this period, trying to escape the new invaders from the East. A good number of Celts had been living in the French cities of Lyon and Bordeaux, where they had once traded tin. They emigrated from France to the British Isles using the Western Seaways.

These Celts brought with them their own form of Christianity. Now Celtic monks, hermits (people who lived alone to devote themselves to God), and pilgrims (travelers visiting churches and other holy sites) began to spread their religion in Wales and Cornwall.

Meanwhile, many other British people had become Christian a long time ago. When Julius Caesar had conquered Britain in the first century A.D., he had inadvertently made Britain more accessible to Christian missionaries. Then, when the Angles and the Saxons forced these new Christians into the western parts of Britain, they took their religion with them.

Finally, in the fifth and sixth centuries, the Catholic Church, which was still based in Rome, began to send priests to England. They wanted to convert the Angles and the Saxons to Christianity as well. While Rome sent priests to England, the Celtic Christians

In small round boats such as this one carrying St. Samson, Celtic missionaries crossed from Ireland, Wales, and Cornwall to the coast of France and Spain and even far out into the North Atlantic. (Authors' archives)

continued to push out to spread their faith. Roving monks and pilgrims used the Western Seaways to reach people who had not yet heard of Christianity.

**The Age of Saints.**  So many people were missionaries at this time, that the period became known as the Age of the Saints. This movement peaked in the seventh century, by which time it had reached Wales, Ireland, Cornwall, Brittany, Scotland, and even some parts of Spain.

The routes of these roving missionaries can be traced by the remains of the churches that they dedicated to their saints. These churches are on coastlines and peninsulas all along the Western Seaways.

The monks and priests also founded *monasteries*, communities where monks live together in religious devotion. St. Samson, for example, founded a famous monastery in Brittany. Celtic Christians founded the mission of Santa Maria de Bretoña in northwestern Spain.

**A New Religion: The Rise of Islam.**  Then in the seventh century, a new religion was founded. The prophet Elijah Mohammed, who lived in Arabia, founded the religion of Islam; the followers of Islam are called Moslems.

Islam grows out of Judaism and Christianity. It recognizes Adam, Abraham, Noah, Moses, and Jesus as prophets of God, but believes that Mohammed is the latest prophet. His book, the *Koran*, is the Moslems' holy book.

Islam spread quickly throughout the Middle East, Asia, and North Africa. In the seventh and eighth centuries, Arab Moslems moved into Spain and southern France. This development stopped the southward spread of Christianity for a time.

Nevertheless, Christian missionaries still pressed northward. Celtic missionaries traveled to Iceland, hundreds of miles in the North Atlantic.

Of course, just because Christian missionaries had reached an area did not mean that everyone there immediately became a Christian. The ancient religions of these peoples were practiced for a long time. But throughout Europe, Christianity continued to spread and become stronger.

## THE VIKINGS

In the ninth century, a new European group began to make raids on other countries around the North Sea and the Baltic Sea. This new group was known as the *Vikings*, which meant *pirates*. The Vikings were great sailors who explored much of the northern world. Their activities greatly affected the use of the Western Seaways.

The Vikings were actually three different groups of people: the *Norse*, or Northmen, from the area that is now called Norway; the *Danes* from what used to be called Jutland and is now called Denmark; and the *Varangians* or the *Rus*, from the area that is now called Sweden.

***The Varangians (Swedes).*** The Varangians concentrated their attention on Eastern Europe. They moved through the Gulf of Finland into the area that is now called *Russia* (named after this invading people, who were also called the *Rus*). There they built the great trading city of Novgorod.

The ancestors of the modern-day Swedes then went south. They opened up the Russian River Routes to the Black Sea and the Caspian Sea. From these routes they traded with the empire of Byzantium (today's Turkey), the country of Persia (today's Iran), and the peoples of Central Asia.

In ships like this one from 800 A.D., the Vikings terrorized coastal Europe for centuries. (By Manning de V. Lee, in Rupert Sargent Holland, *Historic Ships*, 1926)

These Russian River Routes became very important. During the ninth century, there were many different peoples traveling across Europe. Many of them were warlike, conquering the lands that they found and attacking traders and travelers. The land routes were dangerous and disrupted—so the Russian River Routes became the main way to cross Europe. Again, we know this from some detective work done by archaeologists. They have found many Arab coins along the coastline of the Baltic Sea, showing that Arabs and Europeans were trading in this area.

***The Norse.*** The Norse took a different course: they invaded Western Europe. They attacked the northern islands and the lands around the Irish Sea. They moved into the Shetlands and the Orkneys (islands that are today part of Great Britain), using them as bases for their invasion of northern England, Scotland, and Ireland.

The Norse sailed in narrow ships that had only one sail. Instead of depending only on the wind to fill their sails, they also had oars, which sailors used to row the ships.

Because the people in the conquered lands had developed writing systems, they left some records of what it was like when the Norse

Vikings came. Here is one account from 820, written in the *Annals of Ulster* (Ulster is a city in today's Northern Ireland):

> ...the sea spewed forth floods of foreigners over Erin [Ireland], so that no haven, no landing place, no stronghold, no fort, no castle might be found but it was submerged by waves of Vikings and pirates.

By the mid-ninth century, the Vikings began to settle in the Irish cities of Armagh, Dublin, Waterford, and perhaps also Cork and Limerick. During the same period, the Norse and the Irish began to settle in Iceland. Even though many Norse were settling in foreign lands, still more Norse raiders continued to arrive until the early 11th century. After this point the Norse settlers in Celtic lands began to adopt Celtic practices, and eventually adopted the Christian religion of these lands.

***The Danes.*** Danish Vikings invaded different areas. They attacked eastern England and northwestern France. In England, they moved through Kent, East Anglia, and Yorkshire. There they fought with the Angles, the Saxons, and another people, the Jutes. Eventually, the Danish Vikings began to settle in England, and became ancestors of the English today.

The Danes and the Norse also cut deep into Europe, traveling along Europe's many rivers. They pushed down the Rhine, the Seine, the Loire, the Gironde, and the Garonne. A man called Ermantarius, writing in the ninth century, described the effect of the Viking invasions on the cities of France:

> The number of ships grows: the endless stream of Vikings never ceases to increase. Everywhere the Christians are victims of massacres, burnings, plunderings: the Vikings conquer all in their path, and no one resists them: they seize Bordeaux, Périgeux, Limoges, Angoulême and Toulouse [all cities in France]. Angers, Tours, and Orleans [other French cities] are annihilated and an innumerable fleet sails up the Seine [River] and the evil grows in the whole region. Rouen is laid waste, plundered and burnt: Paris, Beauvais and Meaux taken, Melun's strong fortress leveled to the ground, Chartres occupied, Evreux and Bayeux plundered, and every town besieged. Scarcely a town, scarcely a monastery is spared: all the people fly, and few are those who dare to say, "Stay and fight, for our land, children, homes!" In their trance, preoccupied with rivalry, they ransom for tribute [pay off the Vikings] what they ought to defend with the sword, and allow the kingdom of the Christians to perish.

## THE NORMANS

The next set of invaders to have a major impact on the map of Europe was called the *Normans*, descendants of the *Northmen*, or Vikings, who invaded France.

In 842, the Vikings who had come to France decided to spend the winter there, rather than go back home to Denmark for the winter. Gradually, other groups began to settle in France as well. These people became the Normans.

***The Norman Conquest.*** In 1066, the Normans crossed over from France to invade England. They were led by their king William, who came to be known as William the Conqueror after he had conquered England. William had two sons—Robert and William. Robert succeeded his father in Normandy, but William succeeded his father in England where he became the second of a new dynasty of kings in England, and brought a new people into the midst of the Angles, Saxons, Jutes, and Vikings, who had already established themselves in England.

***Other Travels of the Vikings.*** The Vikings headed further south as well, cutting across the Tin Routes. They went as far as Lisbon, in today's Portugal, and Seville, in today's Spain.

In Seville, the Vikings met the Moors—Moslem peoples from northern Africa. The Moors had invaded and conquered Spain, which had been ruled by Christians. Under Moorish rule, Chris-

CIVITATIS BVRDEGALENSIS IN AQVITANEA. GENVINA DESCRIP.

tians, Jews, and Moslems lived together peacefully in Spain for many centuries. The Vikings went as far as to attack North Africa, south of Spain, but ultimately, the Moors remained in control in both places.

Some Vikings settled in southern France, near the ends of the old Tin Routes. Most, however, stayed in northern Europe and gradually adopted Christianity as their religion. As they settled into the lands they had invaded, peaceful trade and travel gradually returned to the Western Seaways.

Medieval Bordeaux built its prosperity on transporting wine to the British Isles and pilgrims to the continent. (From Antoine du Pinet, *Planz*, 1564)

## The Hanseatic Traders

After the Viking invasions, the main focus on the Western Seaways shifted into the Baltic Sea, which marked one end of the trade routes to Russia and the East. Drawn by these attractive markets, German traders began moving around the Baltic in the 12th century. They set up centers all along the seacoast, from Lübeck (in present-day Germany) to Riga (in present-day Latvia).

### The Hanseatic League.

Then a new kind of trade began, under the direction of a new kind of trading group. In the second half of the 13th century, a group of cities on the Baltic and the North seas formed a trade network. The network was named after the *Hansas*—German companies of merchants who dealt with foreign lands. It was called the *Hanseatic League*.

The Hanseatic League was set up to make it easier for cities to beat out their competitors. The cities in the league agreed together on prices and trading practices. They also agreed not to compete with each other—in order to better compete with cities outside their league.

The Hanseatic League was formally set up in 1358. More than 70 German cities became members. In 1370, the league won a trade *monopoly* in Scandinavia (the countries of Denmark/Jutland, Norway, and Sweden). Having a monopoly meant that only cities who belonged to the league were allowed to trade there.

The strongest Hanseatic cities were Lübeck, Hamburg, and Bremen. They were the strongest because they had easy access to either the North or the Baltic seas, where most of the trading was

At major Hansa cities, as in Hamburg (above), crude but effective cranes were used to help load and unload ships. (From *Bilderhandschrift des Hamburgischer Stadtrechts*, 1497, Staatsarchiv, Hamburg)

Staples like the food carried in this Latvian boat were the mainstay of the Hanseatic League's trade. (New York Public Library)

done. However, other Hanseatic cities were river ports deep in the continent, such as Cracow (in today's Poland) on the Vistula River, and Frankfurt (in today's Germany) on the Main River.

Hanseatic traders also pushed overland deeper into Europe. There they met Italian traders, who were coming up from the Mediterranean Sea. These traders helped revive overland trade and travel in Europe.

But it was the sea trade that formed the bulk of the Hanseatic League's activities. Throughout its trading area, Hansa ports supplied warehouses and docks to collect and ship goods. The league also set up depots for its merchants in foreign cities, like London (in modern England), Bruges (in modern Belgium), Novgorod (in modern Russia), and Bergen (in modern Norway).

The trade goods varied according to each port. At London, trade was mainly in wool, lead, and the still-important tin. At Bruges, textiles were the most important, along with metalwork. At Bergen, trade was in salt fish, whale oils, and timber, while Novgorod traders dealt in fur, honey, wax, and flax, as well as luxuries like silks, spices, and pearls from the great trade routes of the south and the east.

***Limits of the Hansas.*** Even though the Hansas were very strong, they never completely controlled trade on the Baltic Sea. And in the 14th century, English and Dutch merchants took a more important role in this trade.

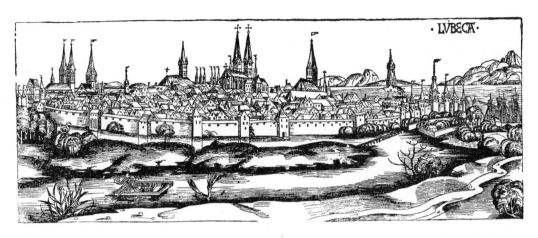

Controlling the portage route across Jutland, Hamburg and Lübeck (above) were the most powerful ports in the Hanseatic League. (From *Schedelsche Weltchronik*, 1493, Greifswald, Universitätsbibliothek)

Part of the expansion was due to an increasing number of places where they could trade their goods. The British had been sending wool to Bruges for a long time, but were now beginning to sell it in Calais, in France, just across the English Channel.

In addition, British and Dutch traders began to move into the Baltic itself. They sailed around Jutland (Denmark) to sell at various cities to the east, especially Danzig (the modern Polish city of Gdansk). British and Norwegian fishermen and traders also became more prominent on the North Atlantic routes to Iceland. Finally, Britain and France both used the old Tin Routes to ship wine and to make pilgrimages.

The Danes realized that there was money to be made from their control of the sea routes around Jutland. In about 1430, they began charging heavy tolls on ships that sailed into the Baltic. At first, this helped the cities in the Hanseatic League, since they could continue to trade by land, so it was to their advantage to have other cities pay huge tolls for traveling by sea.

***The Decline of the Hansas.*** But just as the Hanseatic League seemed to be at its height, several events weakened it.

One major event was the reopening of the Western Seaways from the Mediterranean. For several centuries, the Moslems had controlled Spain and Portugal, as well as North Africa. Thus they controlled both sides of the Strait of Gibraltar, which leads from the Mediterranean into the Atlantic. Under their rule, the Strait of Gibraltar was more or less closed to European traffic and the Atlantic ports in Spain and Portugal were not used very much.

Then, in 1492, the Christian monarchs Ferdinand and Isabella took control of Spain away from the Moslems. They brought in laws to expel all the Moslems and Jews from Spain, so that Spain became a totally Christian country. They also reopened the Strait of Gibraltar to European traffic.

At the same time, Italian city-states were becoming powerful traders further east in the Mediterranean. At the turn of the 14th century, the Italian cities of Genoa and Venice began to send galleys (large boats) through the Strait of Gibraltar and up to London and Bruges. Thus there was even more competition for the Hanseatic traders.

Another major event also weakened the Hansas—a shift in the pattern of migration of the North Sea herring. For some unknown reason, in the early 15th century, these fish stopped migrating to Lübeck and the Baltic Sea, and began to stay in the North Sea. Therefore, the Hansa traders could no longer profit from the sale of these fish. Instead, the Dutch harvested them, which became the basis for their profitable sea trade.

Finally, in the 14th century, a major catastrophe put a stop to the Hansas overland trading. This catastrophe was known as the *Black Plague*, a highly contagious, fatal disease which no one could find a cure for at the time.

The plague was transmitted through the fleas that lived on rats. These disease-carrying fleas could also live on humans and other animals—so that the plague spread wherever people traveled. Al-

Germans fished off the coasts of North and Baltic seas using rods, nets, and traps to catch pike, carp, eels, lampreys, crabs, and other fish. (From *Picture Book of the Graphic Arts*)

most one-quarter of Europe's population was wiped out by this terrible disease. As you can imagine, this severely disrupted trade and travel throughout Europe. And although the Hanseatic League hung on for some time, its power had been broken.

## THE AGE OF DISCOVERY

The Hanseatic League had been based in the North and Baltic seas. During the 15th and 16th centuries, trade around these seas became far less important, while the Atlantic Ocean ports on the old Western Seaways acquired much more importance. From this southwestern part of Europe, ships went even further south and west to explore new trade routes to Africa and Asia. This valuable trade for silks, spices, and other goods became increasingly significant.

At this time, the Italians were the most skilled sailors in all of Europe. However, the Italian cities were not very powerful. In the Middle East, another people, the Turks, were taking over the trade, keeping goods out of Italy. This put many Italian sailors out of work.

So the Italian sailors migrated to Spain and Portugal, where they boarded ships which were sailing along the Western Seaways. At this time, Spain and Portugal were sponsoring explorations for new routes to Africa and Asia. One such famous trip was made by Christopher Columbus, an Italian sailor from Genoa who was sponsored by the king and queen of Spain. Columbus was looking for a new route to India when he discovered the continents of North and South America on his way.

Italian sailors also sailed in northern waters. In 1497, John Cabot, exploring for England, sailed west out of Bristol, and got as far as the coast of North America. John Cabot was originally Giovanni Caboto, an Italian sailor who, like Columbus, was probably born in Genoa.

Although the Italians continued to be good sailors, the Italian cities continued to have problems sponsoring their voyages. By the 16th century, the city of Venice was short of timber and had to have its ships built by the Dutch. Such problems meant that gradually the central focus of the Western Seaways shifted northward, to the English Channel, where the Dutch and British sponsored most of the westward exploring.

This was the period when most of Europe's modern-day ports were being built. Many of the older ports, like Bruges, had gradually

The modern canal from the Mediterranean port of Narbonne followed the line of the old Tin Route as it headed toward the Atlantic. (By A. H. Hallam Murray, in *Sketches on the Old Road Through France to Florence,* 1904)

become silted up, becoming so clogged with mud that they could no longer be used. The Dutch port of Amsterdam gradually took over the role of Bruges by the 17th century. Amsterdam's rise was also fueled by the arrival of many Jews, who had been thrown out of Spain and Portugal in 1492. London and the French port of Le Havre likewise grew in importance in the 17th century.

## MODERN TIMES

Sailors from the Western Seaways explored routes all around the world, beginning in the late 15th century. At first, the explorers were funded by the Spanish and the Portuguese. Later the Dutch, English, and French came to control the new global waterways.

In modern times, the old coastal routes of the Western Seaways have been replaced by routes that cross the oceans themselves. Yet the coastal waters have not been entirely abandoned. All along the coast of Western Europe, fishermen harvest the seas while coastal traders work their way north and south. And for those rich tourists who travel on yachts, the Western Seaways provide a way to sail south, toward the warm and sunny Mediterranean.

Bautier, Robert-Henri. *The Economic Development of Medieval Europe* (London: Thames and Hudson, 1971).

Bowen, E. G. *Britain and the Western Seaways* (London: Thames and Hudson, 1972).

Braudel, Fernand. *The Wheels of Commerce* (New York: Harper & Row, 1979), translated from the French by Siân Reynolds; volume 2 of *Civilization and Capitalism, 15th–18th Century*.

Carpenter, Rhys. *Beyond the Pillars of Heracles: The Classical World Seen Through the Eyes of Its Discoverers* (New York: Delacorte, 1966).

Clark, J. G. D. *Prehistoric Europe: The Economic Basis* (London: Methuen, 1974; reprint of 1952 edition).

East, W. Gordon. *An Historical Geography of Europe*, third edition revised (London: Methuen, 1948).

*Great Rivers of Europe.* (London: Weidenfeld and Nicolson, 1966).

Karmon, Yehuda. *Ports Around the World* (New York: Crown, 1980).

Piggott, Stuart. *Ancient Europe: From the Beginnings of Agriculture to Classical Antiquity* (Chicago: Aldine, 1965).

Pounds, Norman J. G. *An Historical Geography of Europe, 450 B.C.–A.D. 1330* (Cambridge University Press, 1973)

———. *An Historical Geography of Europe: 1500–1840* (Cambridge University Press, 1979).

Stefansson, Vilhjalmur, ed. *Great Adventures and Explorations: From the Earliest Times to the Present as Told by the Explorers Themselves*, revised edition (New York: Dial, 1952).

Tavernier, Bruno. *Great Maritime Routes: An Illustrated History* (London: Macdonald, 1972), translated from the French by Nicholas Fry.

# 2

# THE NORTH ATLANTIC ROUTE

## THE LINK BETWEEN TWO WORLDS

The North Atlantic Route is one of the world's great sea highways. Since the explorers of Europe first discovered the continents of North and South America in the 16th century, the North Atlantic Route has been used to link European and American cultures.

Ships traveling the North Atlantic Route have carried sailors, explorers, fishermen, soldiers, traders, government and church officials, clergy, and a vast flow of emigrants leaving Europe to start a new life in the Americas. Today, the North Atlantic seaway still binds together modern North America and Europe.

The North Atlantic Route first began to be heavily used during the 16th century, when Europeans were exploring, conquering, and settling North and South America. Today, this seaway is by far the most heavily traveled sea route in the world. But this was not always so. During early human history, the North Atlantic seemed to be a vast, bitter sea that led nowhere.

## A COLD AND STORMY SEA

The North Atlantic is one of the world's stormiest seas. Those who sail it have often been at its mercy. Not only is the North Atlantic a stormy sea, it's an icy one as well. The sea is often easy to cross in the summer, but during the winter, some of the cross-Atlantic routes are blocked by ice.

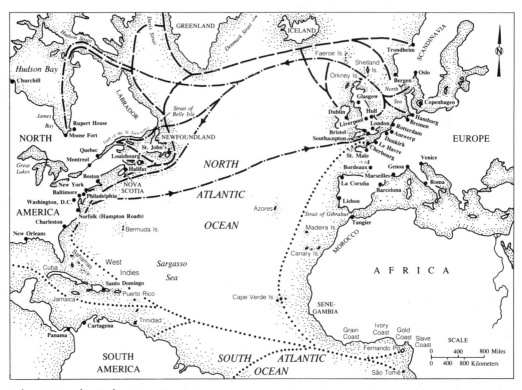

## The North Atlantic Route

——— Early Exploratory Routes ⋯⋯⋯ Slave Trade Routes

—·—·— Later Sailing Routes

***The Geography of the Route.*** When Europeans in the 16th century wanted to sail west to the Americas, they used to set off in the North Sea, which connects the major nations of northwest Europe. From there, sailors would go island-hopping, so that they could put in at safe ports for food and water. If they were leaving from the Norwegian coast, they might stop at the Shetland Islands. If they were leaving from northern Scotland, they would go via the Orkney Islands.

After leaving these islands, the route passes Iceland and cuts south of Greenland. From there, sailors would work their way south along the east coast of North America, moving past Nova Scotia in Canada to the main ports of the United States: Boston, New York, Philadelphia, Baltimore, Norfolk, Charleston, and New Orleans. In fact, many of these cities were founded because they were good ports for this route—natural places for European sailors to stop.

***Winds and Currents.*** When crossing the ocean in a fragile sailing boat, it was important for sailors to know how to use winds and ocean currents to speed their journey. The major current on the North Atlantic is part of a huge circulating system in the Atlantic. Picture a huge circle of water, like a giant whirlpool, spinning between Europe and the Americas in the Atlantic Ocean. One arm of this "whirlpool" spins from the British Isles south past Spain and West Africa; then west to the Caribbean, Florida, and the Bahamas. This part of the current is called the *Canary Current*. The other part of the whirlpool spins up from the Gulf of Mexico, north and east toward Europe. This is known as the *Gulf Stream*.

European sailors did not know about the existence of the Gulf Stream for some time. But when they discovered this important current, they could use it to make the eastward trip from North America to Europe much quicker. As we have seen, the trip from Europe to America was made very far north, in cold and icy seas. The return trip, however, could be made at about the latitude of New England—a much warmer trip!

The Gulf Stream is a very powerful current. Sometimes its very strength caused problems for sailors. If they were traveling west, from Europe to America, they had to be very careful to stay on course. If ice or storms forced them even a little bit south, they were caught in the Gulf Stream—which tried to push them back toward Europe! This was one of the reasons why it took European sailors such a long time to learn to use the North Atlantic Route.

## EARLY EXPLORERS

Even though the heyday of travel on the North Atlantic Route occurred after the 16th century, some explorers in ancient times also traveled on parts of this route. These early explorers may have had to face even more difficulties than the later sailors, because the Earth was actually colder in early centuries. Therefore there was more ice in the northern parts of the ocean, making it harder to travel.

***The Carthaginians.*** The Carthaginians were an ancient people who were originally known as the Phoenicians. Phoenicia was a Middle Eastern civilization located in the land that today is part of the country of Lebanon. The Phoenicians were excellent sailors. They used their knowledge of the sea to expand their power. Eventually, they were forced out of Phoenicia—but by then, they had built other cities in North Africa to which they could flee, such as Carthage, which is located in the area that today is known as Tunisia. They became known as the Carthaginians, after their new capital city.

Early Phoenician (Carthaginian) sailors may have been the first to explore the North Atlantic Ocean. They seem to have traded with people in Cornwall (part of today's Great Britain). Cornish people had tin to trade—and for a while, tin was the only metal that people in Europe and North Africa knew how to use.

The Phoenicians were lucky, because when they were sailing the Atlantic—in the 13th century B.C., the climate was not so cold. It turned cold soon after, and would not warm up again until the 4th century A.D. For all the centuries in between, the North Atlantic sea lanes were blocked by ice.

***The Romans.*** Another great, ancient civilization was that of the Romans. The Roman Empire began as a tiny city on the banks of the Tiber River, in the land that today is part of Italy. From this city, the Romans went on to conquer other Italian cities, then spread even further to conquer most of Europe and a huge part of Asia.

The Romans were not very good sailors. They preferred to travel by land, along the roads they became famous for building throughout Europe and Asia. However, the Roman historian Pliny does tell about the voyage of a Greek sailor named Pytheas. In the fourth century B.C., Pytheas sailed from Massilia (today's French city of Marseilles) through the Pillars of Hercules (today's Strait of Gibraltar), into the open Atlantic. This brave sailor then followed the coast of Europe north, at least as far as northern Britain, and perhaps even further.

Pytheas called the furthest land he reached *Thule*. Pliny and many later historians often called it *Ultima Thule*, meaning the furthest land ever reached by any human. People today still use the phrase "Ultima Thule" to mean "the ends of the earth."

Here is Pliny's description of "Thule," which may be either Scandinavia or some island out in the Atlantic:

> The outermost of all known lands is Thule. At the time of the solstice [the longest day of the year, halfway through the summer], when the sun passes through the sign of the crab, there are no nights there. In winter the days last only a short time, whereas the nights are very long...

Of course, when you go very far north, the days are very long in summer—in the "land of the midnight sun," the sun may even shine at midnight! Likewise, during winter in the far north, the days are very short, sometimes only a few hours long.

**The Celts.**  Unlike the Romans, the Celts were known to be great sailors. The Celts are the ancestors of many European peoples today, including the Irish. Many Celtic sea rovers and monks visited the Atlantic islands, settling there in the seventh century A.D. There seem to have been Irish settlements in Iceland in the seventh and eighth centuries. The Earth's climate was warmer in those days, so it was easier to travel the northern seas.

In records left behind by the Celts, observations similar to those of the Roman writer Pliny are made. Here is how the Irish monk Dicuil described the Faeroe and the Shetland islands when he wrote in 825 A.D.:

> It is now thirty years since clerics who lived in [one of those islands] …from the first day of February to the first day of August told me that not only at the summer solstice, but in the days on either side of it, the setting sun hides itself at the evening hour as if behind a little hill, so that no darkness occurs during that very brief period of time, but whatever task a man wishes to perform, even to picking the lice out of his shirt, he can manage it precisely as in broad daylight. And had they been on a high mountain, the sun would at no time have been hidden from them…

## THE VIKINGS

Ancient and early peoples sailed a little way into the North Atlantic, but the first people to make the trek from Europe to North America were Scandinavians known as the *Vikings*, which meant *pirates*. The Vikings were great sailors who explored much of the northern world.

The Vikings were actually three different groups: the *Norse*, or Northmen, from the area that is now called Norway; the *Danes* from what used to be called Jutland and is now called Denmark; and the *Varangians* or the *Rus*, from the area that is now called Sweden.

The Vikings who explored the North Atlantic were the Norse. By the time the Vikings were active, in the seventh century A.D., the climate had improved enough for the northern sea lanes to become very nearly ice-free. Taking advantage of these new conditions,

Nurtured in the frozen fjords of Norway, the Norse Vikings were well-suited to open the northerly route across the Atlantic. (By Manning de V. Lee, from Rupert Sargent Holland, *Historic Ships*, 1926)

Norse sea-rovers and settlers began to move out across the Atlantic from island to island. This northerly, island-hopping course is an easy one. It is only about 200 miles from Bergen, Norway, to the Shetland Islands, and 200 miles more from the Shetlands to the Faeroe Islands. Then it's 400 more miles to Iceland, and only 200 miles beyond that to Greenland. Sailors were able to take the trip in stages, stocking up with food and water in between.

The Norse Vikings took many years to work their way across to North America. By the late seventh century, Norse emigrants had settled in the Shetlands and the Faeroes, as well as in northern Scotland and Ireland. By the middle of the eighth century, Norse raiders had repeatedly raided these islands.

After the raiders came more settlers. New emigrants settled on islands of the mid-North Atlantic, so sea traffic continued between Norway and the middle of the ocean. Thus the route between Europe and America was opened, partly by intent—but partly by accident. The old Norse *sagas*, or stories, tell many tales of ships being blown off course and into the view of unknown islands, which the adventurous Norse people then explored.

***The Norse in Iceland.*** By the middle of the ninth century, Norse ships began to appear off the island of Iceland. Hundreds and then thousands of settlers left the poor and difficult country of Norway to move to this new land, and by 930 A.D., there were 40,000 Norse people in Iceland. Fifty years after this the Norse started to settle in Greenland.

***Eric the Red.*** One of the most important Norse explorers was known as Eric the Red, because of his bright red hair and red beard. Eric the Red came to Iceland with his father, Thorvald, while he was still in his teens. He went to Greenland sometime in the early 980s. Many Icelanders had probably seen Greenland before Eric did, and some may even have landed there. But Eric actually explored this northern land.

Eric the Red spent three years exploring Greenland. After this initial period of exploration, Eric went back to Iceland, gathered a group of settlers together, and went back to Greenland again, to build the Eastern Settlement.

You can read about Eric's adventures in the Icelandic saga, or story, called the *Saga of Eric the Red*. According to the story, Eric called the new land "Greenland" because "men would be all the more drawn to go there if the land had an attractive name."

***Leif Ericson.*** Eric's son, Leif, was an explorer like his father. When he was old enough, he too went westward, this time to the continent of North America. Leif Ericson (or "Eric's son") was probably the first European to reach North America.

We know about Leif's travels from a group of *archaeologists* (people who study artifacts from the past), who found the remains of an old Viking settlement on the Canadian island of Newfoundland. The archaeologists found that in three of the old buildings, ironworking had taken place. This may mean that this old colony was a ship repair station, possibly for ships exploring the coast of North America.

Besides the Newfoundland settlement, there is not much evidence of Viking exploration of North America. But if we take into consideration that the Vikings made it all the way across the cold and stormy North Atlantic, we may also guess that they may well have sailed down the Atlantic coast.

***Hard Sailing.*** Of course, sailing in this region was far from easy. Here is the way the Icelandic *Saga of Eric the Red* describes one expedition:

> [The explorers] were in high spirits and were pleased with their prospects. But they ran into prolonged difficulties and were unable to reach the seas they wanted. At one time they were within sight of Iceland; at another they observed birds off Ireland. [Imagine how they must have been blown back and forth between east and west!] Their ship was driven back and forth across the Ocean. In the autumn they turned back towards Greenland...worn out by exposure and toil.

In any case, the Norse were the first to open up a sea route across the North Atlantic. Most of that route was in use for a thousand years or so, and is still in use today.

***Colder Climates.*** Only the last 200 miles of the Norse route, from Iceland to Greenland, fell into complete disuse for some time. That was because the northern climate actually became much colder during the 13th and 14th centuries. By the 15th century, the north had become so cold that today we call it the "Little Ice Age." (The first Ice Age was a time many centuries B.C., when much of the Earth was frozen or covered by glaciers.) During the "Little Ice Age," even the routes between Iceland and Norway were often blocked by ice. Icelanders who had been used to getting food from Norway then depended on dried codfish from English fishing boats for part of their food supply.

When the climate worsened, the Greenland settlements fell on hard times. New settlers did not want to go to this cold and frozen land, and the settlers who were there faced harsh conditions. European exploration in North America halted, until the voyages of Christopher Columbus and other Italians in the late 15th and early 16th centuries.

## EXPLORING THE AMERICAS

***Explorations of the Renaissance.*** The late 15th and early 16th centuries were an exciting time in Europe. Historians have called that time the *Renaissance*, or "rebirth," because there seems to have been a rebirth of interest in pushing forward the limits of knowledge, exploration, art, and new ideas in all areas. Scientists and explorers were challenging old ideas about the geography of the world, astronomy, and physics, while artists were rediscovering the Ancient Greek techniques of portraying human form.

Part of the reason that there was so much exploration during the Renaissance was the great expansion of merchant activity. Merchants had been trading for spices, silks, jewels, and other beautiful goods with Arabic traders, who traveled back and forth between Asia and Europe. At the beginning of the Renaissance period, Europeans began to become more interested in traveling to Asia themselves. European explorers began to wonder how they might sail to India, China, and the Spice Islands of Indonesia and Malaysia.

Imagine what the world looked like to an educated European of the Renaissance. There was the known world—the countries of northern and southern Europe, and North Africa on the south border of the Mediterranean Sea. And then there was the unknown world—the vast uncharted oceans that led to unknown lands. Europeans were aware that somewhere out there, there were China, India, and the other Eastern countries whose spices and silks they procured from other traders. But they did not know how to picture the entire geography of the world. They did not know the shape of Africa, or where Africa and Asia were located in relation to Europe.

To make matters more complicated, many educated people of the time did not believe the world was round. The ancient Greeks had believed this for a time, but during the Middle Ages (the period before the Renaissance, from about the 5th century to the 15th century), most people believed that the Earth was flat. During the Renaissance, the theory of the round Earth came back again.

Columbus believed in this theory, and so he speculated that if he sailed to the *west*, sooner or later he would end up in the *east*. He would have been right—except that the continents of North and South America were in his way!

**Explorers North and South.** It is not surprising that the cold North Atlantic discouraged explorers. Columbus and others preferred the mid-Atlantic, using the southern half of that ocean's currents.

Columbus was an Italian sailor who sailed from Spain. Many Portuguese sailors also explored the south- and mid-Atlantic, sailing around Africa in their effort to find a way east. However, in the 16th century, the climate of the northern regions began to grow warmer. And northern Europeans—the Dutch, British, and French—also wanted to explore routes east.

For these northern Europeans, Columbus' route was not very convenient. Columbus had sailed across the Atlantic at about the latitude of Bermuda. But northerners found this too southerly a path which took them the long way round. If you look at a map, you can see that for the northerners it was far easier to sail straight across to Canada's Gulf of St. Lawrence, rather than to follow the Canary Current. This becomes even clearer when you remember that northerners left from Bristol or Liverpool, England; and from Brittany and Le Havre in France.

It is interesting to note that Lisbon, which is so far south in Europe, is at about the same latitude as New York and Philadelphia. Yet Lisbon is much warmer than these American cities—in fact, it

Bristol, shown here in 1673, was the home port of many early British explorers of the Atlantic. (City Archives of Bristol)

has almost a tropical climate. That's because the Gulf Stream flows up from Mexico toward the west coast of Europe, warming the entire area of Western Europe. True, the Gulf Stream does flow by the east coast of North America, but it travels too far off the coast to warm up our cities.

## The Northwest Passage

Southern European sailors finally found a route to the east. They discovered the Cape of Good Hope Route, around the southern tip of Africa. But this route was both too long and too far south to be practical for northern Europeans. They sought a route known as the *Northwest Passage*, a route that was supposed to cut through along the north coast of North America to reach Asia.

We now know that this passage did not exist. Before the Panama Canal, there was no way to sail from the Atlantic to the Pacific unless you sailed up north into the Arctic Ocean (or around the tip of South America). Obviously, this Arctic route was too cold and too frequently blocked by ice to be a practical pathway for trade or travel. However, searching for the Northwest Passage helped push Europeans to explore the Arctic Ocean and the northern part of North America.

Explorers searching for the Northwest Passage helped to open up North America to trade and travel for other Europeans. Explorers such as Cartier and La Salle were looking for the Northwest Passage—and discovered furs and other valuable trading goods. While looking for the Northwest Passage, Cartier opened up what became French Canada and La Salle followed the great Mississippi River all the way to the Gulf of Mexico.

Likewise, early explorers for England such as John Cabot, Martin Frobisher, and John Davis sailed the Atlantic coast of North America, looking for a way through to the Pacific. Remember, these men had no idea how large the continent of North America was. Nor did they have any idea what its shape was, or where its rivers led.

A major Dutch explorer, Henry Hudson, found Hudson Bay while he was looking for the Northwest Passage. Hudson's ship was eventually lost in the cold northern seas of Canada while he was searching for a way through to the Pacific. Later fur traders used Hudson's discovery of the bay. They were able to sail from Europe right into the western side of the bay, from where they controlled the fur trade of western Canada.

Throughout the 1800s, many people explored the far north. But it took until 1903 for an expedition to actually sail from the Atlantic to the Pacific. Roald Amundsen, a Norwegian explorer, found the Arctic Ocean route that Henry Hudson and so many others had sought in vain.

As you can imagine, the passage through the Arctic Ocean was cold and dangerous. In the 1940s and 1950s, huge icebreakers did make it through more easily than the sailing ships of the past were able to do. Even so, the Northwest Passage is still more dream than reality. The North Atlantic Route, from Europe to North America, proved to be far more important.

## North Atlantic Trading

***Trading for Fish and Furs.*** When the first big wave of European explorers reached North America after Columbus' famous voyage of 1492, they were disappointed. They had wanted to reach India, China, or some other Far Eastern land where they could trade for rich goods. They did not want to find North America, which had none of the spices or silks that they were seeking. They soon realized, however, that North America could also be a profitable source of trade. Instead of simply being an obstacle on the way to the East, North America became an end in itself.

By the beginning of the 16th century, large numbers of fishing boats from Portugal, Britain, Brittany (in northern France), and the Basque country (in southern France and northern Spain), were harvesting the waters of the Grand Banks, off New-foundland. These fishermen dried their cod on shore and traded with the local Native Americans for furs.

From then on, trade in fish and fur grew by leaps and bounds. The fur trade lasted into the 19th century. The fish trade across the North Atlantic continues to this day.

***The Dangers of the North.*** The explorers of the North Atlantic had many dangers to deal with. One of the worst was the thick fog of this misty northern land. The French sailor Marc Lescarbot, traveling off Newfoundland in 1601, left this description:

> [We]...fell to the fogs again, which [from afar] we might perceive to come and wrap up about, holding us continually prisoners three whole days for two days of fair weather they permitted us.. Yea, even divers [various] times we have seen ourselves a whole sennight [seven nights, or a week] continually in thick fogs, twice without any show of sun.

Another danger of the northern Canadian coast was rocks. The Atlantic coast has many rocks that stick unexpectedly out into the water, and these rocky points are dangerous to ships traveling at night or in the fog. Many capes along the North Atlantic coast have carried the name "Graveyard of Ships."

Nevertheless, exploration continued. Europeans recognized that the North American continent could be profitable in many ways, and they continued to push on by land and sea.

## THE ATLANTIC MIGRATION

***Settlers in a New Land.*** The fishermen and explorers who had kept the North Atlantic Route open in the early 16th century were gradually joined by settlers. Many people wanted to leave Europe for various reasons.

Some people felt that they could find more opportunity in what they called the "New World." The Native Americans living in North America had their own societies and cultures, but sometimes they were willing to trade with Europeans, or to allow Europeans to hunt, trap furs, or develop farmland. In other cases, Native Americans did not welcome Europeans, but the continent was big and the Europeans had superior weapons. A man who could not buy land in Europe might be able to do so in North America.

Some people came to North America for religious reasons. The Puritans, for example, practiced a religion that was not welcomed in England. They began a colony in North America where they were free to worship as they pleased. Ironically, they themselves were not interested in providing religious freedom for others, for they believed that their way was the correct one.

At first, the migration to North America went slowly. In 1600, a full century after the explorer John Cabot first landed on the North American continent, there were only a few hundred French settlers and traders in Canada. The British had yet to found the colony of Virginia.

By 1650, a strong flow of British settlers across the North Atlantic had begun. At this time, there were 20,000 people in Virginia and 30,000 more in New England. The climate had begun to get warmer, and settlers were more willing to come to the slightly warmer lands of New England.

By 1700, British North America had a population of 280,000. Of these, 100,000 had come across the Atlantic from Europe, 10,000 had been brought forcibly from Africa as slaves, and the rest were North American–born.

The flow of emigrants from Europe became stronger and stronger. During the 19th century, many Scottish, Irish, and German settlers came to North America, and, until the early part of the century, more slaves were brought in.

***A Difficult Passage.*** The trip across the North Atlantic was not an easy one. Until the 1820s, North Atlantic travel depended primarily on sailing ships. These had to fight the winds and the currents as they traveled from Europe toward America. The trip from Europe to America took over two months—twice as long as the return trip from America to Europe.

Emigrants from Europe were often barely able to afford the cheapest ticket to the New World. They traveled in *steerage*, the lowest part of the ship, and the least comfortable. Imagine how much a sailing ship would pitch and toss on a stormy North Atlantic sea. Passengers below were often seasick. In addition, the crowded travelers had to cope with lice, poor sanitation, and the lack of fresh food and water. The ships were also a breeding ground for every kind of disease, including typhus and cholera. Of the 89,738 people who left the British port of Liverpool for Quebec in 1847, some 15,330 people died either en route or shortly afterward in Canadian hospitals.

Here is one emigrant's description of the voyage in steerage from Liverpool in that year:

> Before the emigrant has been a week at sea he is an altered man. How can it be otherwise? Hundreds of poor people, men, women, and children of all ages, from the drivelling idiot of ninety to the babe just born, huddled together without light, without air, wallowing in filth and breathing a fetid [stale, foul] atmosphere, sick in body, dispirited in heart, the fever patients lying between the sound [healthy], in sleeping places so narrow as almost to deny them the power of indulging, by a change of position, the natural restlessness of the disease; by their ravings disturbing those around, and predisposing them, through the effects of the imagination, to imbibe [drink in] the contagion; living without food or medicine, except as administered by the hand of casual charity, dying without the voice of spiritual consolation, and buried in the deep without the rites of the Church. The food is generally ill-selected and seldom sufficiently cooked, in consequence of the insufficiency and bad construction of the cooking places. The supply of water, hardly enough for cooking and drinking, does not allow washing. In many ships filthy beds, teeming with all abominations, are never required to be brought on deck and aired, the narrow space between the sleeping berths and the piles of boxes is never washed or scraped, but breathes up a damp and fetid stench...
>
> The meat was of the worst quality. The supply of water shipped on board was abundant, but the quantity served out to the passengers was so scanty that they were frequently obliged to throw overboard their salt provisions and rice ... because they had not water enough for the necessary cooking and the satisfying of their raging thirst afterwards. They could only afford water for washing by withdrawing it from the cooking of their food. I have known persons to remain for days together in their dark, close berths because they thus suffered less from hunger...

## TRADE IN THE NORTH ATLANTIC

Besides carrying people, ships in the North Atlantic also carried a huge quantity of goods. However, the infamous "triangle trade" carried both.

***The Triangle Trade***. This route, popular into the early 19th century, used the circulating currents of the Atlantic to avoid the northern routes and make increased shipping profits. Ships took goods from America to Europe using the Gulf Stream and the west winds. Then they sailed south with the wind and the Canary Current to West Africa, where they picked up "cargoes" of slaves, who had been captured by Europeans, Arabs, or sometimes by other Africans looking to profit from the European trade. From Africa, ships sailed westward with the wind and the current, to reach the Caribbean and the American South. There they sold slaves to plantation owners, and bought sugar, molasses, rice, cotton, or other American products—which they carried back to Europe. Ironically, the products they picked up were mainly grown by the labor of the very slaves whom they had sold.

***Northern Atlantic Trade.*** Traffic was always heavy on the northern westbound route, as well. As the English colonies in North America grew, so did a large trans-Atlantic trade. The colonies sold cheap raw materials to Britain, and bought back expensive finished products manufactured in British workshops and factories. This unbalanced trade at this time brought huge profits into Britain at America's expense.

Colonies of all kinds have suffered from this unbalance in the 18th, 19th, and 20th centuries, and the American colonies were no exception. Their disadvantage continued even after the American Revolution of 1776, when the new United States won its political independence from Great Britain.

***The Cotton Gin and the Industrial Revolution.*** In 1793, Eli Whitney invented the cotton gin, a machine that made it possible for one person to pick more cotton than ever before. This was good news for the slaveholders who owned large plantations, for they greatly expanded their production of cotton, using slaves to do the picking. They also pushed the plantation system—in which one person held large sections of land and many slaves—far out into the Mississippi Basin.

The British were happy to buy as much cotton as the United States could supply, for they were undergoing the *Industrial Revolution*. The Industrial Revolution was the process of building and developing factories and machines so that unskilled, cheap labor could manufacture goods in large amounts. Eventually, most countries in Europe and North America went through this process, but Britain was the first to go through it.

British textile factories now had machines that could weave cloth much faster than weavers had been able to do by hand. To keep the weaving machines busy, the factories needed the cotton grown in the United States. By the time of the Civil War, the U.S. supplied half of Britain's cotton. Meanwhile, people in the United States bought the finished cloth that the British made, as well as other manufactured British goods. This trade—raw materials from the one side, finished products from the other—was carried on across the North Atlantic, in the sailing ships of the first half of the 19th century.

In the infamous "triangle trade," Europeans brought slaves from Africa to the Americas, then followed the Gulf Stream home with colonial goods. (From *La Commerce de Amerique par Marseilles,* 1764)

## Packet Ships

The sailing ships of the North Atlantic trade were usually called *packets*. They were "workhorse ships"—big, strong, with square sails or rigging ("square-rigged ships"), tough enough to withstand the pounding waves of the North Atlantic. Even when they were fully loaded, they could fight their way across the ocean currents, often in the teeth of a *gale*, or sea storm.

In the early years, the North Atlantic ships had no regular schedule. They would wait for enough mail, passengers, and cargo

to make their trip profitable. Then their owners would give the signal and off they sailed.

***The First Shipping Lines.*** However, starting in 1818, a more regular travel began. Packets traveling on the North Atlantic became "liners" or units in shipping "lines," which ran scheduled sailings from port to port. These lines had their own names: the Black Ball Line, the Black Star, the Red Star, and the Black X. Once scheduling began, it became very popular with traders and travelers, who liked to know that they could count on a ship to leave at an appointed time. Liners became the main carriers on the North Atlantic Route.

These packet ships, compared to earlier vessels, were huge. They weighed 1,000 tons and had several decks. Luxury passengers paid for a place on the expensive upper decks. Emigrants bought the cheaper tickets for the upper holds (storage areas), also known as "'tween decks" (between decks) or "steerage" (because they were so near the ship's steering gear). The cargo was stored in the very lowest holds. When the packet ships traveled east, from America to Europe, they carried mainly luxury passengers. Instead of people, cargo was stored in the "'tween decks" area.

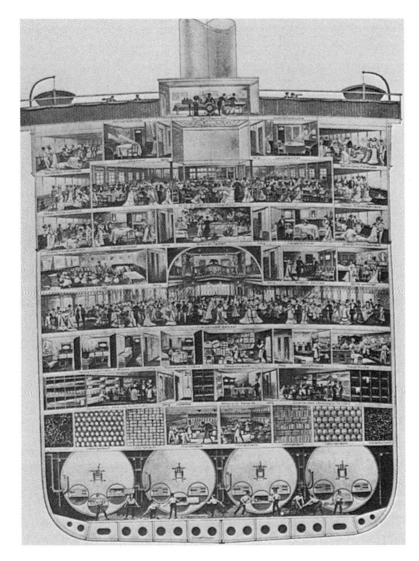

This cross-section of the Hamburg-America Line's steamer, *Amerika*, shows how its 2300 steerage passengers were crammed into bunks, above the cargo deck but below the cabin deck and the luxurious upper decks. (Hapag-Archiv, Hamburg)

Eventually, ship construction had improved so that packet ships could make faster trips. By the mid-19th century, the average time across the North Atlantic was 36 days for those going west, and 24 days for those going east.

## THE AGE OF STEAM

In 1818, a ship called the *Savannah* crossed the Atlantic powered by steam rather than wind. This new method of travel meant that

This Georgia ship, the *Savannah*, had steam-powered paddles along with sails, for her cross-Atlantic voyage in 1819, but the steam engines were later removed. (The Mariners Museum, Newport News, Virginia)

ships could travel more quickly, more safely, and more surely across the stormy Atlantic. By the middle of the 19th century, huge steamships were sailing from every major port in Europe to every major port in America.

Steam travel took several years to develop. The *Savannah* was actually a sailing ship that was assisted by steam, and was very much ahead of its time on the North Atlantic Route. Steam was, however, regularly used on the lakes and rivers of North America before steam became commonplace on North Atlantic crossings.

***The Cunard Line.*** In 1840, Samuel Cunard's British and North American Royal Mail Steamship Company started a swift, regular trans-Atlantic service that quickly replaced sailing ships on the North Atlantic completely. The Cunard line launched the *Britannia*, the first of four ships built with British government help for the Liverpool-North America run. This was the ship that truly began the Age of Steam on the world's oceans.

The British author Charles Dickens crossed on the *Britannia* in 1842, two years after it had been put into service. He described his sleeping quarters as:

> ...an inaccessible shelf they called a sleeping berth [with] a very thin quilt covering an equally thin and very flat mattress, utterly impractical and quite preposterous, which I thought at first was merely a cheerful jest [joke] on the part of the ship's owners and captain.

If Dickens thought his "shelf" was a bad joke, he should have seen the conditions in steerage. These early steamships were not much larger than the ocean-going tugboats of today, in the 1,000-ton class of the sailing packet ships. To a below-decks passenger, steam seemed at first to bring little improvement.

But soon steamships were making the east-to-west run faster and more surely than sailing ships, even though they too had to fight the current. By the 1850s, the Collins and Cunard ships were regularly making the run in 10 or 12 days.

***Larger and Faster Ships.*** Eventually the size of the steamships grew so that they could carry more people far more comfortably, both above deck and in steerage. These new ships also carried more cargo. By the late 1850s, reliable ships were being built in the 3,000- to 4,000-ton range. The days of the packet ships were over.

For a while, sailing ships continued to sail to Europe, and they continued to be used on the long trip to Australia as late as the 1940s, since it was difficult for steamships to carry enough coal to last the whole journey. Even today, sailing ships are still used to carry large amounts of cargo on some routes. But on the North Atlantic, with its special needs, the Age of Steam came quickly.

## The Great Liners

Ships continued to become bigger and faster. By the late 1870s, some 8,000-ton ships could make the crossing in seven days. By 1897, Germany's 14,350-ton *Kaiser Wilhelm der Grosse*, then the largest liner in the world, made the westbound crossing from Southampton, England, to Sandy Hook, New York, in only five days and 22 hours. It made the return trip in a speedy five days, 15 hours, and 10 minutes—only 60 years after Cunard had started the age of steam on the North Atlantic.

In the 20th century, the pace of change grew even more quickly. In 1906, the *Mauretania* and the *Lusitania* were launched. They were 30,000-ton superliners that crossed the Atlantic in just under five days.

Ships continued to get bigger and bigger. A new generation of ships was designed to set new standards of speed, safety, and luxury. Even steerage passengers on some of these ships had a relatively comfortable and stable trip.

***Hardships in Steerage.*** Nevertheless, for the millions of European emigrants seeking work or land in the United States and Canada in the early 20th century, the trip was generally crowded, dirty, and miserable. True, there were ships steaming out of every major port of Europe, with modern science to aid their fight against swift currents and stormy seas. Yet for those who had never before traveled on the open waters, a steerage crossing was often remembered like this:

It was so rough! Oh God, it was so rough! I didn't see a thing. A lot of time you just lay in your bed when you don't feel so good. You don't get up and go because if you do, you get dizzy and then you get worse sick, because the water was so rough. That was rough weather—in November, winter starts. Oh, the waves! Oh God! I thought the ship would turn over, but it didn't...

The *Titanic*, thought to be unsinkable, was sunk by an iceberg on its maiden voyage from Southampton, England, to New York in April 1912. (Steamship Historical Society of America, Inc.)

That description was the account of a Ukrainian immigrant named Mary Zuk, who in 1912 crossed to America in a 20,000-ton steamship. She was supposed to be making a safe trip. Yet perhaps she had heard of the tragedy of the *Titanic*, a 45,000-ton ship which only six months earlier had hit an iceberg and sunk, with a loss of over 1,500 lives.

## MODERN TIMES

The North Atlantic continued to be the main highway between Europe and North America. In both the First and the Second World Wars, people and goods continued to flow across this well-traveled sea; however, the travelers were soldiers and the goods were war materials. Hundreds of thousands of people died in battles in the North Atlantic. Thousands of ships and later hundreds of submarines were lost there.

The years between World War I and World War II were the age of the superliners for passenger travel. In 1935, the 79,300-ton *Normandie* offered luxury and speed on its ocean crossing. In 1938, it was joined by the 80,750-ton *Queen Mary*. These ships offered recreation, luxurious sleeping quarters, and many meals a day to the first-class passengers traveling between Europe and the United

Past Ellis Island (far right), the Statue of Liberty (upper left), and Castle Garden (lower left), this liner—the *Imperator*—is steaming out of New York harbor and back to Europe for more immigrants. (Library of Congress)

States. After World War II, a few new luxury liners were built, such as the *United States* and the *Queen Elizabeth II*. Most people, however, preferred to take the quicker journey by air. The days of the passenger superliners were over.

***Commercial Trade and Travel.*** Today the pathways of the North Atlantic are still busy, but now these sea lanes are primarily concerned with commercial traffic. Massive shiploads of cargo travel both ways across the Atlantic. Only a few travelers, drawn by the romance of the great liners, keep alive the North Atlantic's memory as one of the great passenger routes of bygone days.

## Suggestions for Further Reading

Armstrong, Warren. *Atlantic Highway* (New York: John Day, 1962).

Briggs, Peter. *Rivers in the Sea* (New York: Weybright and Talley, 1969).

Brownstone, David M., Irene M. Franck, and Douglass L. Brownstone. *Island of Hope, Island of Tears* (New York: Rawson, Wade, 1979).

Denison, A. D. *America's Maritime History* (New York: Putnam's, 1944).

Jones, Gwyn. *The Norse Atlantic Saga* (London: Oxford, 1964).

Jones, Maldwyn A. *Destination America* (New York: Holt, 1976).

Leip, Hans. *River in the Sea* (New York: Putnam's, 1958).

Maxtone-Graham, John. *The Only Way to Cross* (New York: Macmillan, 1972).

Morison, Samuel Eliot. *The European Discovery of America: The Northern Voyages* (New York: Oxford, 1971).

Mowat, Farley. *Westviking* (Boston: Little, Brown, 1965).

Parry, J. H. *The Age of Reconnaissance* (New York: Praeger, 1969).

———. *Trade and Dominion* (New York: Praeger, 1971).

———. *The Discovery of the Sea* (New York: Dial, 1974).

———. *Europe and the Wider World, 1415-1715* (London: Hutchinson, 1949).

Penrose, Boies. *Travel and Discovery in the Renaissance, 1420-1620* (New York: Atheneum, 1975).

Silverberg, Robert. *The Challenge of Climate* (New York: Meredith, 1969).

Villiers, Alan. *Wild Ocean* (New York: McGraw-Hill, 1957).

# 3
# THE ST. LAWRENCE-GREAT LAKES ROUTE

The European explorers of the 16th century were seeking a pathway to the riches of the Far East. For centuries, they had been trading for spices, silks, jewels, and beautifully made ornaments from China, Japan, India, Malaysia, Indonesia, and other Asian lands. These goods had been brought to Europe by Arab traders. European traders became anxious to find their own route to the East since they would then be able to get hold of these precious goods more cheaply, without having to go through a middleman.

In 1492, the Italian explorer Christopher Columbus sailed west from Spain. The Spanish monarchs, Ferdinand and Isabella, sponsored his voyage. Columbus was following an old theory of the Greeks—that the world was round. If he sailed west long enough, he reasoned, sooner or later he would end up in the east. Columbus would have been right except for two miscalculations. One—the world was much larger than he imagined. To round the globe from Spain to Japan was a far longer journey than he anticipated.

Columbus' second miscalculation was even more unexpected: he didn't know that the continents of North and South America lay between Europe and Asia. Columbus' voyage to America was followed by several other European explorers, who found out more about these newly discovered continents.

51

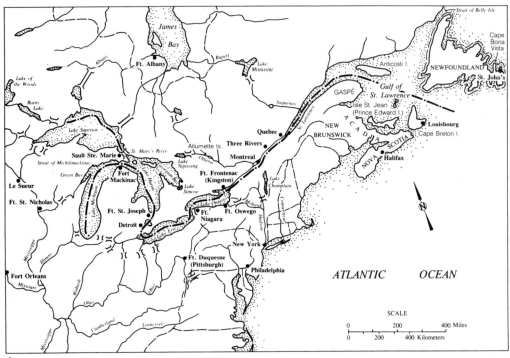

## The St. Lawrence-Great Lakes Route in the Mid-18th Century

—·—·— Main St. Lawrence-Great Lakes Route ———— Boundaries of English Settlements

⊐⊏ Main Portages

Once the Europeans knew about North America, they changed their plans slightly. They still wanted a fast route east—but now, they thought, they would have to go through North America somehow. Perhaps there was a series of rivers or lakes that they could use to sail from the Atlantic to the Pacific? At this time, the Europeans had no idea how large North America was. Nor did they know anything about its shape or geography. They continued to hope that there might be a *Northwest Passage*, a passage through Canada that would lead to the Pacific.

In fact, the only way to cross North America by water is to go via the Arctic Ocean, an extremely cold and dangerous journey. The European explorers of the 16th and 17th centuries never found a way through this fabled passage. What they did find, ironically, was a rich continent that might yield even greater profits than if they had sailed straight to India. Samuel de Champlain, John Cabot, Jacques Cartier, Henry Hudson, and many other explorers laid the basis for the European conquest of North America through their voyages to this continent.

One of the major gateways to North America was the St. Lawrence River, which leads to the continent's inland seas. The St. Lawrence River and the Great Lakes system became the key to the riches of North America, as explorers entering Canada penetrated to the heart of the vast land.

## EARLY TIMES

***Carthaginians, Greeks, and Celts.*** The Europeans of the 16th century were not the first to visit North America. We don't know much about the earliest history of this area, but we do know that by 330 B.C. the Carthaginians may have visited Iceland. Perhaps they went even further west and reached the North American continent itself. Likewise, ancient Greek sailors may have made the western trip.

Later, a people called the Celts (ancestors of many present-day Europeans, especially the Irish) may have visited Iceland as early as 300 A.D. They seem to have settled in Iceland by 750–800 A.D., and to have stayed for a century or so.

***The Vikings.*** In about 850 or 875 A.D., a people called the Norse, or Northmen, came to Iceland. The Norse who came were known as *Vikings*, or pirates. They were good sailors with strong ships who made raids on many other parts of Europe, including England and France. They settled in many places, including Iceland, the most northwest part of Europe.

About a century later, in 980 or 990 A.D., the Norse living on Iceland went even further west to explore Greenland. This expedition was probably led by the great Icelandic explorer, Eric the Red. The Icelanders liked Greenland, and started a colony there.

Until the end of the 14th century or so, Greenland had healthy settlements of thousands of people. Then the northern climate grew colder throughout the 14th and 15th centuries, only warming up in the 16th century. This cold weather made life in the north far more difficult. Most of the Greenlanders abandoned their homes. When John Cabot, exploring for England, landed in Greenland in the 16th century, he found only ruins of earlier settlements. Perhaps, though, there were some other settlements that he did not find, that seem to have survived well after he and Columbus reached the North American mainland.

***How Far Did the Vikings Go?*** Something that historians are still arguing about is how far past Greenland the Vikings managed to go. They certainly got as far as Newfoundland, which today is part of Canada. We know this because in the 1960s, archaeologists discovered the remains of a Viking settlement at L'Anse aux Meadows, in northern Newfoundland.

But did the Vikings go even further? Did they use their Newfoundland settlement as a base to explore the west? Many historians think they did. Eric the Red's son, Leif Ericson, visited a place he called Vinland. Perhaps this was on the coast of New England; or it might have been in northeastern Canada. Unfortunately, we don't really know whether the Norse people actually came onto the North American continent itself, so we still don't know who were the first Europeans to reach North America.

## THE AGE OF EXPLORATION

***The Renaissance.*** The Europeans who came to North America in the 16th century were very adventurous. They were living during a period of time that historians have called the *Renaissance*, or "rebirth." They used this name because at this time there was a great rebirth of interest in science and exploration. Traditional ideas about anatomy, astronomy, physics, and geography were suddenly being challenged. Scientists and explorers were demanding that no one take any idea on faith any more, but that every idea be open to a new interpretation. At the same time, artists were reassessing the theories of the Ancient Greeks about using anatomy to show a realistic portrayal of the human body.

Added to this atmosphere of excitement and exploration was the growing economic power of merchants and traders. These people were eager to profit from trade with the Far East, and ready to help finance explorations that might make such trade easier and faster.

***Explorers South and North.*** In the south, the Portuguese explored the continent of Africa, which was just as unknown to them as North America was. The Spanish sent Columbus westward, where he discovered the islands of the warm Caribbean. Both were looking for routes to China, India, and the Spice Islands—both

Starting in 1534, Frenchman Jacques Cartier explored the St. Lawrence River, gateway to North America. (Engraving from a painting in The Town Hall, St.-Malo, France)

found new continents which would profit them greatly over the centuries.

Meanwhile, in the north, the British, the French, and the Dutch were exploring northerly routes across the Atlantic. British merchants from Bristol backed the voyage of John Cabot in 1497. Actually, Cabot was born Giovanni Caboto. He was an Italian sailor who had come to England because the Italians could no longer afford to finance the long trips that interested him. The British sent him north to find a passage to the east. With the possible exception of the Vikings, Cabot was the first European to touch the continent of North America.

The French sent Jacques Cartier out of the city of St.–Malo, in Brittany, in northern France. Cartier sailed in the spring of 1534. He was the first person to explore the Gulf of St. Lawrence and to enter the river itself. His voyage was financed by the king of France, who gave him this mission:

> ...[to] make the voyage...to the new lands, to discover certain isles and countries where there is said to be found a vast quantity of gold and other rich things.

Of course, the king wasn't talking about Canada; he was talking about China and India. But interestingly enough, his words did become relevant for what Cartier eventually discovered in Canada.

## Into North America

***The Geography of the St. Lawrence.*** What Cartier found and began to explore is the great water route into the heart of North America. Even today, ships crossing the Atlantic enter the St. Lawrence River from the northeast, since it is at the end of the shortest and best way across the Atlantic from northern Europe.

From the Atlantic Ocean, the great river cuts through the rugged Appalachian Mountains, which run north-south and which block the route by land into the center of the North American continent.

Once it has flowed beyond the mountains, the St. Lawrence opens out into the great, linked inland seas—the five Great Lakes. The Great Lakes make it possible to sail around the heartland of North America, reaching many areas safely and easily by water, rather than having to carry cargo over land.

Finally, the lakes link up with the huge Mississippi-Missouri River system. Thus, you can sail into the St. Lawrence River and make your way all the way south down to the Gulf of Mexico, or into the midwestern and southern United States.

You can imagine how important this water system must have been in the days before cars and trucks and paved roads. Carrying cargo and trading goods was much more easily done by water than overland, for the waterways were natural roads, and ships did not have to be hauled by oxen or drawn by horses.

The first people to use the St. Lawrence-Great Lakes system were the French. With it, they were quickly able to reach, explore, and claim the whole center of the continent. Meanwhile, the English were still hemmed into the narrow coastal strip between the Atlantic Ocean and the Appalachian Mountains. There was no easy land route which traversed the Appalachians.

***Native Americans in North America.*** There was one other water route through the mountains. The Mohawk Trail led up the Hudson River and west through the Mohawk Valley. But in the 16th and 17th centuries, this area was still occupied by the Mohawk Indians. The Mohawks were one of five nations that banded together to form the *Iroquois League* or the *Iroquois Confederacy.* In 1570 they had joined with the Oneida, the Onondaga, the Cayuga, and the Seneca, for mutual protection against the European invaders.

The Iroquois League was so powerful that the British did not attack them. Instead, they signed a treaty in which the British agreed not to settle in the Mohawk Valley, or go west on the Mohawk Trail. Because of this treaty, the Iroquois fought with the British during the American Revolution. The treaty was respected until the British lost the American Revolution. After that, settlers began to go west along the Mohawk Trail.

## THE FRENCH

***Explorer Jacques Cartier.*** The French were exploring the heartland of North America throughout the 16th and 17th centuries. As we have seen, Jacques Cartier was the first. In 1534 he sighted Cape Bonavista, on the southeastern coast of Newfoundland. He sailed north along the coast, and went into the Gulf of St. Lawrence through the Strait of Belle Isle (which means "beautiful island"), between Newfoundland and the Quebec mainland. From here he went further into Canada, exploring this new area, until finally he went back to France.

The next year, he made a second voyage. This time he was guided by two Native Americans whom he had taken captive on the first voyage. They were able to guide him into the St. Lawrence River, on which he sailed to the Native American village of Stadacona. Later, the Europeans named this spot Quebec City. Cartier went further, to the Native American village of Hochelaga, which the Europeans later conquered and named Montreal. The name "Montréal" comes from the French name for a local mountain, which the British called "Mount Royal."

Cartier climbed Mont Réal and looked down from the great height to see the Lachine Rapids. He finally understood that he would not be able to sail through on the St. Lawrence to China and India.

***French Settlers.*** For the French, the St. Lawrence River was more than a gateway to the continent. It became the main center of French settlement and power in North America. It was also a local road. For well over a hundred years, it was the only real road used by the traders and colonists who followed Cartier out of France. Imagine having to walk or ride through miles of unexplored woodland, with no real paths or protection from wild animals. Now think how much easier it would be to sail along a wide river, once you knew where that river led and could count on finding river towns to stop in along the way. Thus, the French came to depend on the St. Lawrence River.

By the mid-1660s, 130 years after Cartier's voyages, there were a few thousand French settlers in North America. Most were living along the St. Lawrence valley, especially in or near Quebec. They held long riverfront farms, which could usually only be reached from the water.

Then, in 1663, French colonists began to make land routes instead of simply depending on the St. Lawrence. They cleared the area from Quebec City to Montreal. Finally, they began to build roads and settlements in areas a little back from the river.

## THE FRENCH SETTLE IN NORTH AMERICA

The exploration of the St. Lawrence River and the Great Lakes continued. Some explorers were still seeking the Northwest Passage. But others realized that there was money to be made right there in North America—from the fur trade.

***The Fur Trade.*** Much of the history of the French exploration of the continent is also the history of the fur trade. The French, the British, and finally the American colonists trapped and traded for beaver and other furs over the 16th, 17th, and 18th centuries. Before the arrival of the European explorers, the Native Americans had trapped only what they needed for fur and meat. Suddenly Europeans were trapping in huge numbers and shipping the pelts back to Europe to make hats and coats. Naturally, the size of the population of fur-bearing animals began to decrease. Fur traders and trappers followed these animals all the way from the St. Lawrence over the Rocky Mountains and on to the Pacific Ocean.

Not until the 19th century did canals like this one around the Long Sault Rapids begin to tame the St. Lawrence. (Public Archives of Canada)

***Exploring the River.*** The French explorers and trappers were greatly helped by their use of the light, very durable birchbark canoe. Canada's native peoples used such canoes to ride west on the shallow, swift rivers of the area. A canoe 20 to 25 feet long was light enough for two people to *portage*, or carry overland, in order to cross the areas where the rivers did not run, or where the waters were too shallow for a boat. Yet this light canoe was strong enough to carry many travelers and much cargo through the water. It was also easy to maneuver, and so could be used on a stream that would not be deep enough or smooth enough for a heavier boat.

In 1670, Father René Galinée described these canoes and what they meant to the early French *voyageurs* (voyagers, or fur traders) and explorers:

Navigation above Montreal is quite different from that below. The latter is made in ships, barks, launches, and boats, because the River St. Lawrence is very deep, as far up as Montreal, a distance of 200 leagues; but immediately above Montreal one is confronted with a rapid or waterfall [the Lachine Rapids] amidst numerous large rocks, that will not allow a boat to go through, so that canoes only can be used.

These are little birchbark canoes, about twenty feet long and two feet wide, strengthened inside with cedar floors and gunwales, very thin, so that one man carries it with ease, although the boat is capable of carrying four men and eight or nine hundred pounds' weight of baggage. There are some made that carry as many as ten or twelve men with their outfit, but it required two or three men to carry them.

This style of canoe affords the most convenient and the commonest mode of navigation in this country, although it is a true saying that when a person is in one of these vessels he is always, not a finger's breadth, but the thickness of five or six sheets of paper from death... It is only the Algonquian-speaking tribes [that is, American Indian nations that spoke Algonquian languages, including the Arapaho, the Cree, Delaware, Blackfeet, Cheyenne, Ojibway/Chippewa, Shawnee, Illinois, Michigan, and MicMac peoples] that build these canoes well...

The convenience of these canoes is great in these streams, [which are] full of cataracts and waterfalls, and rapids through which it is impossible to take any boat. When you reach them, you load canoe and baggage upon your shoulders and go overland until the navigation is good; and then you put your canoe back in the water, and embark again...

To avoid the rapids on the left, this 15-man birchbark canoe is being put ashore; some goods are already being transported on the portage in the right background. (By W. H. Bartlett, from N. P. Willis, *Canadian Scenery*, 1842, New York Public Library)

## EXPLORER SAMUEL DE CHAMPLAIN AND HIS COMPANIONS

The French explorer Samuel de Champlain made a series of voyages that opened up the North American heartland. Cartier was the man who found the way into the St. Lawrence River—but Champlain is the explorer who used that river to explore the Great Lakes and the rivers beyond.

In the spring of 1613, three-quarters of a century after Cartier had arrived, Samuel de Champlain began his series of voyages, starting on the Ottawa River. He sailed on this river past the Long Sault Rapids and the site of modern Ottawa (the capital of Canada), going as far as Allumette Island.

Then, in 1615, Champlain went even further. He went up both the Ottawa and French rivers, and sailed all the way to Lake Huron, one of the five Great Lakes. On the way back, he traveled with a war party of the Huron nation and reached another Great Lake, Lake Ontario. Champlain joined the Huron attack on a village of the Onondaga nation, which was further south, at Lake Oneida (a lake that today is in upstate New York). The Hurons lost this battle and went back north—and Champlain went with them, returning to Quebec the way he had come.

Another explorer, named Etienne Brulé, traveled with Champlain on this voyage, but he broke off from the party at Lake Simcoe. Then Brulé went to the western end of Lake Ontario and from there to the south shore of a third Great Lake, Lake Erie. Brulé's expedition lasted five years, and he is thought to have explored much of the Great Lakes region, including the fourth Great Lake, Lake Superior.

Finally, Jean Nicolet, who had also traveled with Champlain, embarked on another voyage in 1634. Nicolet went all the way to the western end of Lake Huron. From there, he passed through the Strait of Michilimackinac, and on into the last Great Lake to be explored by the Europeans—Lake Michigan. Nicolet sailed along Lake Michigan's north shore, all the way to what is now the city of Green Bay, Wisconsin.

## ROBERT DE LA SALLE DISCOVERS THE MISSISSIPPI

Champlain and his companions opened up the Great Lakes to European travelers. The next significant step in the discovery of

North America was taken by Robert de La Salle, who discovered the Mississippi-Missouri River system that links northern Canada with the southern United States, from the St. Lawrence River to the Gulf of Mexico.

In 1668, La Salle made it to the far western end of Lake Ontario. Eleven years later, in 1679, he went further still, sailing on the St. Lawrence into the Great Lakes system, and crossing four of the five Great Lakes from end to end.

Finally, La Salle linked up with the Mississippi River. This was his greatest discovery. He began on the north shore of Lake Ontario. From there he sailed past the mouth of the Niagara River and on past the Niagara Falls. Other Europeans had seen this great waterfall by then. But it was still an amazing sight. Father Louis Hennepin was traveling with La Salle. He has left us this description:

> Betwixt the Lake of Ontario and Erie, there is a vast and prodigious Cadence of Water which falls down after a surprising and astonishing manner, insomuch that the Universe does not afford its Parallel. 'Tis true, Italy and Suedeland [Sweden] boast of some such Things; but we may well say they are but sorry Patterns, when compar'd to this of which we now speak.
>
> At the foot of this horrible Precipice, we meet with the River Niagara, which is not above half a quarter [or one-eighth] of a League broad, but it is wonderfully deep in some places. It is so rapid above this Descent, that it violently hurries down the wild Beasts while endeavouring to pass it to feed on the other side, they not being able to withstand the force of its Current, which inevitably casts them down headlong above Six hundred foot.
>
> This wonderful Downfall is compounded of two great Cross-streams of Water, and two Falls, with an Isle sloping along the middle of it. The Waters which fall from this vast height, do foam and boil after the most hideous manner imaginable, making an outrageous Noise, more terrible than that of Thunder; for when the Wind blows from off the South, their roaring may be heard above fifteen Leagues [about 45 miles] off.

La Salle sailed past Niagara Falls to the place that today is the city of Buffalo, New York. There he built a ship of about 30 tons, the *Griffin*. This was the first vessel other than a canoe to sail the Great Lakes—unless the Vikings had done so hundreds of years before.

The *Griffin* carried 34 men along Lake Erie, Lake Huron, and Lake Michigan, all the way to Green Bay. From there, La Salle sent the ship back with a load of furs. But the *Griffin* never reached the

The Niagara Falls has always been a place of striking beauty, but to early travelers it was also a major barrier on the St. Lawrence-Great Lakes Route. (From *Nouvelle découverte d'un très grand pays...entre le Nouveau Mexique et la Mer Glaciale,* Utrecht, 1597)

fort at Niagara. It was lost without a trace and has never been found. La Salle, however, went on with his journey. Traveling by canoe again, he went south to the foot of Lake Michigan, passing the place that is now Chicago. He then went on to the Mississippi River.

La Salle was not the first French explorer who had reached the Mississippi. The Jesuit missionary, Father Marquette, and Joliet, had reached this river six years earlier. But La Salle is the one who set the pattern for travel through the Great Lakes onto the Mississippi. Later that route was extended to connect with the St. Lawrence River, from the heart of North America out into the Atlantic Ocean.

## TRADERS AND MISSIONARIES

***Native Americans and Europeans.*** Native Americans lived in the whole area that the Europeans were exploring for the first time. They had their own cultures and customs, their own ways of life. The Europeans were not interested in becoming integrated into the Native American world. For the most part, they had three main things they wanted from the Native Americans: help with exploration; trade for furs; and European missionaries sought to convert the Native Americans to Christianity.

The Native Americans reacted to the European invasion in various ways. Sometimes out of friendliness or fear, they helped the Europeans to explore the continent. Sometimes, as we have seen, they made treaties with the Europeans against rival or hostile Native American tribes. They also began trapping animals and trading furs with the Europeans.

However, often the Native Americans resisted the Europeans and their strange ways. Although the Europeans considered the native peoples "savages," Native Americans actually had very well-developed systems of government and religion. They proved to be good warriors, defending their land and their customs against the French and the British. From the 16th century through the 19th century, Europeans and U.S. residents had to take notice of the rights of Native Americans, making treaties when they could not conquer them in battle.

Despite outbreaks of hostility with Native Americans, the Europeans continued to trade with them, and European missionaries continued their efforts to convert them to the Christian religion. All this activity continued as the European exploration proceeded.

***Lake Superior.*** As the French moved west along the Ottawa River and Lake Huron, they also continued to explore Lake Superior. The first French explorer on Lake Superior was probably Etienne Brulé in 1620. By 1678, French explorer Daniel Duluth had explored the western end of the lakes. This route through Lake Superior bypassed the country governed by the Iroquois League, avoiding conflict with this powerful group of Indian nations.

North of Superior, however, the French set up both trading posts and *missions*—churches and schools where priests came to convert Indians to Christianity. Missionaries of the *Jesuit* branch of Catholicism had been arriving in the Lake Superior country from the early 1640s. By the 1660s, there were missions on the south shore of the lake as well.

In 1668, Father Marquette founded a mission at Sault Ste. Marie. Five years later, he and Louis Joliet went on to explore the Mississippi. Meanwhile, the famous trapper Pierre Radisson explored the northwest shores of Lake Superior in the early 1660s.

By the end of the 17th century, the main outlines of the St. Lawrence-Great Lakes Route were set. But there were still political problems in dealing with the Iroquois, who did not want trade to be carried on along the south shore of the Great Lakes.

In addition, there were political conflicts between two European nations, the British and the French. These two peoples fought for control of the St. Lawrence River and the Great Lakes system, for they recognized that these waterways were the key to mining the riches of North America and carrying rich furs back across the Atlantic to their home countries in Europe.

*The French and Indian Wars.* Between 1679 and 1763, the French and the British fought a series of battles that came to be known as the French and Indian Wars, for the French and the Indians often fought together against the British. Many of the battles were fought along the St. Lawrence-Great Lakes Route, including battles at Fort Niagara, and at Louisbourg, the Nova Scotia fortress that guarded one of the main passages from the North Atlantic into the Gulf of the St. Lawrence.

Finally, in 1759, the French and British fought one of their greatest battles, on the Plains of Abraham in Quebec. In 1760 the great French city of Montreal finally fell to the British, who maintained political control of Canada until that country's independence

The taking of Quebec, in the Battle of the Plains of Abraham, was a crucial event in the establishment of English domination in Canada. (Public Archives of Canada)

many years later. The French-speaking and English-speaking residents of Canada still sometimes quarrel over which language should be the official language of any province.

## THE ENGLISH IN CANADA

After the British took control of Montreal, they became the major European power in North America. The Europeans on the St. Lawrence River, from Montreal eastward, were still mostly French—as they are to this day. But British influence became much stronger. The names of many old French towns or forts became anglicized, or were changed altogether. For example, the French Fort Frontenac in Ontario, named for the explorer Frontenac, had its name changed to Kingston (or "King's town"), and this name persists to this day.

Under the English, the St. Lawrence-Great Lakes Route was no longer the main route west. The British preferred to take the Trans-Canada Route west from Ottawa, a more direct land-based route. After the American Revolution of 1776, when 13 British colonies declared their independence from England, the British stuck to the Trans-Canada Route even more. This was because the St. Lawrence-Great Lakes Route formed the border between the independent United States and the colony of Canada, and the English did not want to travel on the border.

Before canals were built at Sault Ste. Marie, Michigan, goods and even whole boats were carried over the neck of land, in the 1850s on a horse-powered railroad. (Great Lakes Historical Society)

***Bottlenecks Along the Route.*** There were some physical problems that had to be solved before the St. Lawrence-Great Lakes route could be used to its fullest potential. The St. Lawrence, for most of its course, is a wide, easily navigable river, and can be used by ocean-going ships for almost 1,200 miles, from the Strait of Belle Isle to Montreal. But after this point the 200-mile passage between Montreal and the eastern end of Lake Ontario was much more narrow and shallow.

Further on into the lakes there were other bottlenecks. For example, no ship could sail over Niagara Falls! At this point in the route, ships had to unload their cargo, which had to be carried over land until the next body of water below the falls. This was expensive and difficult. The neck of land separating Lakes Huron and Superior at Sault Ste. Marie was another portage that acted as a bottleneck. Nevertheless, strong trade continued to grow along the St. Lawrence-Great Lakes Route.

***The Canals Are Built.*** During the early 19th century, a great period of canal-building began. And with the building of the canals

The city of Buffalo linked New York's Erie Canal with the St. Lawrence-Great Lakes Route. (Lithograph by J. H. Colen after drawing by John W. Hill, Buffalo, N.Y., 1852-53, Buffalo Historical Society)

came a period of great increase in traffic on the St. Lawrence-Great Lakes Route.

Much of that growth was due to the building of the Erie Canal in the United States. The Erie Canal was finished in 1825, connecting Lake Erie and the Mohawk River. Even though this canal was not part of the St. Lawrence-Great Lakes system as such, it brought large numbers of people and great amounts of trade to Buffalo and to Lake Erie. During the rest of the 19th century, several more canals were built. In 1825, the Lachine Canal bypassed Montreal's Lachine Rapids. In 1832, the 126-mile-long Rideau Canal connected Ottawa to Kingston, on Lake Ontario. The first American Sault Ste. Marie Canal was completed in 1855, and the first such Canadian canal was completed in 1895. Together these two toll-free passages formed one of the busiest canals in the world.

By the end of the 19th century, it was possible for large ocean-going vessels to move freely up the St. Lawrence as far as Montreal. And lake vessels could move freely between all the Great Lakes ports. But there was still one large obstacle: traveling between Montreal and the Great Lakes.

Finally, in 1959, the St. Lawrence Seaway was completed. Then it became possible for ocean-going ships to move freely all the way from the Atlantic Ocean into the heart of North America, to Duluth, Chicago, Detroit—2,300 miles away from the great ocean to the east. The St. Lawrence Seaway was now one of the most heavily traveled inland waterways on earth.

And so the voyage begun by Cartier was completed—not to China and the Spice Islands as was originally intended, but to the far richer land at the end of the inland seas. Today, people from all over the world come to see the ocean-going ships passing through the massive locks of the St. Lawrence-Great Lakes Seaway.

## SUGGESTIONS FOR FURTHER READING

Barry, James P. *Ships of the Great Lakes* (Berkeley: Howell-North, 1973).

Browne, George Waldo. *The St. Lawrence River* (New York: Putnam, 1905).

Burpee, Lawrence J. *An Historical Atlas of Canada* (Toronto: Nelson, 1927).

———. *The Discovery of Canada* (Toronto: Macmillan, 1944).

Creighton, Donald. *A History of Canada* (Boston: Houghton Mifflin, 1954).

Cumming, W. P. et al. *The Exploration of North America* (New York: Putnam, 1976).

Curwood, James Oliver. *The Great Lakes* (New York: Putnam, 1909).

Guillet, Edwin C. *The Story of Canadian Roads* (Toronto: University of Toronto Press, 1966).

Hatcher, Harlan. *The Great Lakes* (London: Oxford, 1954).

Hatcher, Harlan, and Erich A. Walter. *A Pictorial History of the Great Lakes* (New York: American Legacy Press, 1963).

Hills, T. L. *The St. Lawrence Seaway* (New York: Praeger, 1959).

Josephy, Alvin M. *The Indian Heritage of America* (New York: Knopf, 1969).

Malkus, Alida. *Blue-Water Boundary* (New York: Hastings House, 1960).

Morison, Samuel Eliot. *The European Discovery of America: The Northern Voyages* (New York: Oxford, 1971).

Mowat, Farley. *Westviking* (Boston: Little, Brown, 1965).

Munro, William Bennett. *Crusaders of New France* (New Haven: Yale University Press, 1918), volume 4 in the Chronicles of America Series.

Parkman, Francis. *France and England in North America* (London: Faber & Faber, 1954), edited by Samuel Eliot Morison.

———. *LaSalle and the Discovery of the Great West* (Boston: Little, Brown, 1897).

Wrong, George M. *The Conquest of New France* (New Haven: Yale University Press, 1918), volume 10 in the Chronicles of America Series.

# 4

# THE TRANS-CANADA ROUTE

## CROSSING CANADA

In 1534, French explorer Jacques Cartier entered the St. Lawrence River and began the European exploration of Canada. Two hundred and fifty-nine years later, in 1793, British explorer Alexander Mackenzie finished the European journey from east to west, arriving at what we now call Vancouver Island in the Pacific Ocean.

Proud of his journey, Mackenzie wrote his name and the date and a short message in large letters in vermilion [red dye] and grease on a huge rock in Dean Channel. Another British explorer, George Vancouver, found the message a few days later:

> Alexander Mackenzie, from Canada by land, the twenty-second of July, one thousand seven hundred and ninety-three.

Mackenzie was part of a process that spanned three centuries, the European exploration of Canada and indeed of all North America. In the early 16th century, the Europeans sent many expeditions around the world, looking for quick and easy passages to China, India, and the Far East, where they hoped to trade for spices, silks, and jewels. Instead, they discovered the continents of North and South America.

These continents were ultimately a greater source of profit to the Europeans than the Far East was. But for many years, the Europeans did not realize the potential gains to be reaped from the Americas. They continued to search for an easy way to get from the Atlantic to the Pacific to tap into Far Eastern trade. In the course of this

71

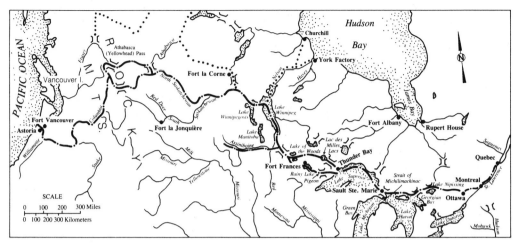

## The Early Trans-Canada Fur Trade Routes

—·—·— Main Trans-Canada Route        ⊨    Main Portages

········· Other Main Fur Trade Routes

search, they explored much of Canada and developed the Trans-Canada Route.

## TWO WAYS WEST

***Europeans and the "New World."***   Think of what the world must have looked like to the Europeans of the 16th and 17th century. They were familiar with the geography of Europe, of course. And they knew that "somewhere out there" were China, India, and the other places where their spices and silks came from. What they did not know was that the continents of Africa and North and South America lay between them and Asia. And when they discovered these continents, they did not immediately know how big they were, how they were shaped, or how much of an obstacle they might be to further travel east.

Thus the exploration of Canada was partly a search for a way to open up the west to Europeans, so that they could profit from the rich fur trade of this new land. And later, of course, the exploration was an effort to open up the fertile farmland to European settlers, who cut down the forests where Native Americans lived and set up a new way of life.

For many years, however, Europeans were motivated by a search for the *Northwest Passage*, a possible sea route from the Atlantic to the Pacific. In their search, they learned much about the geography of Canada.

***Westward Across Canada.*** There are two ways west across Canada. One way follows the St. Lawrence River to the Ottawa River, and then goes on to Lake Superior, the most northerly of the Great Lakes. This is the St. Lawrence-Great Lakes Route (see Chapter 3).

Beyond the Great Lakes, however, the route crossed difficult, marshy land dotted by many smaller lakes. With no natural pathway to follow, no river or waterway, early travelers generally angled northwest toward Lake Winnipeg. Once out of the lake country, they made their way across the Canadian plains, whose flat and well-drained surfaces made much better ground for traveling.

Eventually explorers made their way to the Rocky Mountains, a difficult journey indeed. On the far side of the Rockies, travelers linked up with the Columbia River system, which they followed down to Vancouver and the Pacific Ocean. This was the route that the first explorers forged—the Trans-Canada Route. Later, Canadians developed this route into roads and railroads.

## THE EARLY FRENCH AND THE NATIVE AMERICANS

The early French explorers believed that they were entering a "new world." In reality, of course, they had found a land that Native American peoples had inhabited for many years. Although the French considered these native peoples "savages," the native peoples had their own systems of government and their own religions.

The native population understood very well the land where they lived and how to travel in it. They had invented birchbark canoes that were light enough to carry overland where necessary but strong enough to hold several people and several hundred pounds of cargo in difficult rivers. They had also developed "canoe trails" that connected eastern and western Canada.

From the first, Europeans counted on trade and assistance from the Native Americans. The first European to land in North America (with the possible exception of the Vikings) was John Cabot, an Italian sailor financed by the British. Cabot reached Canada in 1497 and started active fish trade between Europeans and Native Americans along the North Atlantic coast.

The French explorer Jacques Cartier landed in Canada in 1534, having discovered the St. Lawrence River's entryway into the continent. When Cartier entered Chaleur Bay on the coast of New Brunswick in 1534, he was met by:

> …two fleets of Indian canoes that were crossing from one side to the other, which numbered in all some forty or fifty canoes. Upon one of the fleets reaching this point, there sprang out and landed a large number of Indians, who set up a great clamour and made frequent signs to us to come on shore, holding up to us some furs on sticks…

The native Americans consisted of many different tribes and nations, who had developed treaties and trading systems amongst themselves. The Hopewell culture, for example, was centered in the Ohio Valley, but traded across the continent in shells from the Gulf of Mexico, obsidian (a hard, shiny black stone) from the west, and copper and lead from the Lake Superior region. Even in the 16th century, when the French were beginning to push westward, Native Americans continued to trade copper on their great routes.

When the Europeans entered the North American continent, they tried to cut in on this trade. At the mouth of the Saguenay River,

This is one artist's view of Jacques Cartier and his party arriving in Canada. (Painting by Peter Sullivan, adapted from the Vallard map, Public Archives of Canada)

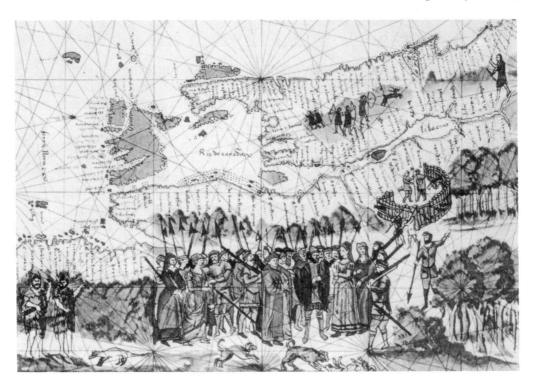

where the St. Lawrence widens from a river to a gulf, they Europeans established a trading base where they exchanged their tools for Native American furs. Furs were brought out from deep in the heart of the continent, traveling from nation to nation to reach the Europeans. In turn, Indian nations traded European tools among themselves, passing them far into North America.

***The Iroquois League.*** Many native peoples were friendly with the Europeans, trading with them and helping them to explore the land. One group of nations, however, was not so friendly. This was the Iroquois League, a group of five native peoples who had banded together for protection against the Europeans. In 1570, the Mohawk, Oneida, Cayuga, Onondaga, and Seneca joined forces to present a united front to the Europeans. In 1722 they were joined by the Tuscarora. The Iroquois saw the Europeans as a threat. And at this time, they were powerful enough in their own right to resist that threat. Since the 13th century, the nations that later formed

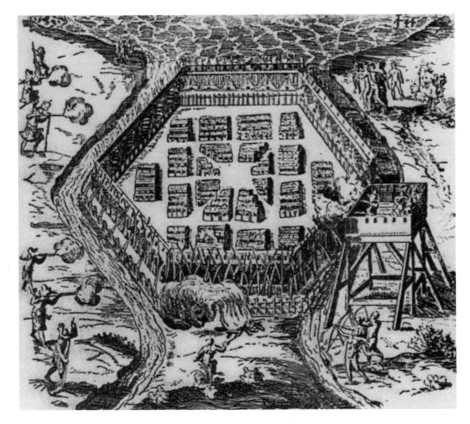

When the French arrived in the St. Lawrence Valley, they found Native American settlements like this Iroquois fort. (Engraving after a drawing by Samuel de Champlain, from his *Voyages et Descouvertures faites en la Nouvelle France,* 1619)

the league had been moving east from the Mississippi Valley. By early in the 17th century, they held much of the country south of the Great Lakes and east to the Hudson River and Lake Champlain. They kept the French out of the southern Great Lakes and away from the land routes south of the lakes. Thus, most European trade and travel was forced northward for many years.

**The French vs. the British.** There were two great European powers active in the northern North America at this time—the French and the British. The British were mainly confined to the narrow strip of land between the Atlantic coast and the Appalachian Mountains. The French were luckier. They had discovered the St. Lawrence River and its connection with the five Great Lakes. These waterways gave them access to all of North America—except the parts that the Iroquois controlled.

Thus, the Iroquois and natural geography forced the creation of the Trans-Canada Route. When the French wanted to go south, they could sail through the Great Lakes and onto the Mississippi-Missouri River system down to the Gulf of Mexico (see Chapter 3). When they wanted to go further west, they sailed on the Ottawa River out of Montreal, rather than taking the difficult waterway between Montreal and Lake Ontario.

## THE FUR TRADE

Eventually, the French and the British gave up on finding a northwest passage to the Pacific. By this time, however, they had realized how valuable the fur trade could be. The beavers of North America had been caught by Native Americans for fur and for meat, but in very small numbers. The Europeans, however, began "harvesting" the beaver, killing huge numbers and sending back their skins to Europe to make hats and coats. Eventually the beaver became quite scarce—but not before trappers had followed it all the way to the Pacific for over two or three centuries.

The French explorer Samuel de Champlain was very important in opening up the St. Lawrence-Great Lakes Route into Canada and what would later be the United States. Champlain was also trying to develop the fur trade. In his search for new supplies of beaver, he arranged to meet the Huron Indians, who became the middlemen in the trade. They got the furs from other nations, then traded them to the British.

Champlain and others continued to push westward into Canada, primarily along the rivers and lakes that became part of the St. Lawrence-Great Lakes Route (see Chapter 3).

***The British Enter the Picture.*** In the mid-1660s, the British entered into trade on the Trans-Canada Route. Ironically, it was their enemies, the French, that made this possible. The French explorers Pierre Radisson and Médard fell into disagreement with the French government in Quebec. So they went to England and met with King Charles II in order to obtain his sponsorship.

Radisson and Chouart excited Charles II about the possible profits to be made in the Canadian fur trade. This all led to the formation of the Hudson's Bay Company, which was to have a powerful influence on the development of western Canada. Radisson convinced the English that there were enormous profits to be made in the fur trade. He especially recommended a base on Hudson's Bay, in the territory controlled by a Native American nation, the Cree.

At many portages in western Canada, like this one at Kakabeka Falls, travelers placed rows of logs in the ground to ease hauling. (By William Armstrong, *Canadian Illustrated News*, 1871)

British fur trade traffic, here at Fort Edmonton on the Saskatchewan, was dominated by the all-powerful Hudson's Bay Company. (Confederation Life Association)

Radisson pointed out that with a base on the bay, there would be no need for middlemen to bring furs out from the heartland. The trading post would be right in the center of where the trapping took place.

Radisson described Cree country and its people like this:

> We went from Isle to Isle all that summer. We pluckt abundance of Ducks, as of all other sort of fowles; we wanted nor fish nor fresh meate. We weare well Beloved, and weare overjoyed that we promised them to come with such shipps as we invented...
>
> They [the Cree] are a wandering nation, and containeth a vast countrey, in winter they live ye land for the hunting sake, and in summer by the water for fishing. They are of a good nature...and are [more] satisfied than any others that I knewed. They cloath themselves all over with castors' [beavers'] skins in winter, in summer of staggs' skins. They are the best huntsmen of all America, and scorn to catch a castor in a trappe.

Radisson had worked out that fur traders operating from Hudson's Bay would be able to profit greatly by eliminating Native American middlemen. They could also ship furs and trade goods directly by sea to Europe. The Hudson's Bay Company did just that, trading out of the towns York Factory and Churchill, which were both on Hudson's Bay. The company operated profitably from the 1670s onward.

## THE FRENCH IN WESTERN CANADA

The French continued into the 18th century to develop a route across Canada, going north and west beyond Lake Superior. Daniel Duluth, a French explorer, had built a trading post at the mouth of the Kaministikwia River, at what is now Thunder Bay on Lake Superior. From there, French trappers and traders began to explore the country leading out to Lake Winnipeg and the Great Plains.

Their progress was slow. This was because beyond the Great Lakes, the country was very difficult to traverse, without a single major water route west. Nevertheless, the French persevered. The last of the great French traders and explorers was Pierre Gaultier de Varennes, Sieur (or Lord) de la Vérendrye. During the 1730s, he and his sons journeyed to Lake Winnipeg, to Portage la Prairie, and northwest to link up with the main Native American-English trading routes west from Hudson's Bay. La Vérendrye built a series of trading posts in western Canada. One was at the mouth of the Assiniboine River, at what is now Winnipeg. Others were on the Saskatchewan, Winnipeg, and Red rivers, and at Rainy Lake, Lake of the Woods, and Lake Manitoba.

La Vérendrye also went far south, to the country of the Mandan nation on the Missouri. He was seeking a water route west along the Missouri, but he didn't find it. The U.S. explorers Lewis and Clark would later find a route, and would follow it to the Pacific. But even though La Vérendrye sent his sons all the way out into Yellowstone country, he was unable to find a path westward beyond the plains.

La Vérendrye also found and used a more southwesterly route past Lake of the Woods to Rainy Lake and out into the Great Plains. Perhaps La Vérendrye was successful because he was advised by a local Native American guide. He went south from the Kaministikwia to the Pigeon River and then west on the Pigeon through the Grand Portage to Rainy Lake. This Grand Portage route west roughly followed what is now the Canada-United States border. For some time, this route was the main choice of westbound travelers in Canada.

The British Go West

Trappers and traders would open up the West as they followed fur-bearing animals like these Rocky Mountain beaver. (From Maximilian, Prince of Wied Nu-Wied, *Travels in the Interior of North America in 1832-4*)

# THE BRITISH GO WEST

While the French were opening up the Canadian plains from the south, the British were carrying on some modest explorations of their own. August Kelsey went west on the plains out of York Factory in 1690. He apparently went as far as the Saskatchewan River, perhaps even to the Assiniboine. His intention was "to discover and bring to commerce" a western nation, perhaps the Mandans.

Other British explorers went further after La Vérendrye. Anthony Henday explored westward out of York Factory in 1753–1754. He traveled into the country of the powerful Blackfeet, and spent the winter with them. Unlike the Indians further east, who sailed in canoes and fished, these plains people rode horses and lived by hunting buffalo. However, they were not sure that they wanted to trade with the Europeans, for they were not interested in leaving their land.

The potential rewards from the fur trade were very great. Thus in the half century after Henday and La Vérendrye, the great plains (now Manitoba, Saskatchewan, and Alberta) were thoroughly explored and mapped. And the British built forts and trading posts across western Canada, claiming their right to trade and trap on this land. At this time also, the exploration of the Rockies and the Arctic was beginning.

## THE BRITISH TAKE CANADA

While the French and British explorers were pushing westward in search of valuable furs, their two countries were battling for control of North America. The French had explored the inland waterways and won the support of many of the Indian nations. The British, however, had superior military forces.

***The French and Indian Wars.*** The two countries fought several battles between 1689 and 1763 which came to be known as the French and Indian Wars because of the Indian support for the French. Finally, the British were victorious and took political control of Canada. This victory changed the role and the direction of the Trans-Canada Route.

Before their victory in 1763, the British had held the east coast of the entire continent, from north of Florida all the way up to Newfoundland. The British Hudson's Bay Company had held the entire north country, in a large arc extending outward from Hudson's Bay. The French, however, had held the inland waterway systems, but now the British took control of this area as well.

After this time the British explorers and traders rapidly began ousting the French. They moved out along the main southern Trans-Canada Route from Montreal, Ottawa, and the Great Lakes, as well as from Hudson's Bay. The French "voyageurs" (voyagers, or fur traders) were still there, but the leadership, finance, and ownership of the fur trade came from the British.

In 1795, the British organized a second company, the Northwest Company, which operated out of Montreal. This company took over the old French routes and grew to control three-quarters of the fur trade. Tremendous competition developed between the new Northwest Company and the old Hudson's Bay Company. Both companies sent explorers west to find new sources of fur and other trading goods. This greatly speeded the European exploration of western Canada. Over the next 25 years, both companies established far-flung networks of trading posts and forts throughout the

Canadian west. Several Native American nations were still living in that region which was the reason for the British building forts. However, for the most part, the Europeans were successful in either subduing the Native Americans or involving them in trade.

***The Rockies.*** The last barrier between this westward expansion and the Pacific Ocean was the Rocky Mountains. The first explorer to successfully forge a route over them was Alexander Mackenzie, who was the first to reach the Pacific Ocean by land, in 1793. However, Mackenzie's route proved to be not very practical for later explorers. He had started down a terribly difficult river (later named the Fraser River), and then abandoned that route to cut across country. Most traders and settlers would not want to use such a difficult route.

In 1808 another explorer, Simon Fraser, set out from Fort George, on the eastern slopes of the Rockies. Fraser explored the same river that Mackenzie began on, which was later named the Fraser River in his honor. Like Mackenzie, Fraser found the river's rapids quite frightening:

This immense body of water passing through this narrow space in a turbulent manner, forming numerous gulfs and cascades and making a tremendous noise, had an awful and forbidding appearance.

Many trappers brought their furs to Fort Vancouver, where they sold them to the Hudson's Bay Company. (Authors' archives)

Fraser and his party could find no portage route—no place to carry their boats and cargo overland. So they had to sail right through the rapids. In fact, as they continued down the Fraser River, they had to sail through many rapids—a difficult and dangerous trip! Eventually, they too reached the Pacific Ocean at what is now Vancouver. But Fraser's route was also not very practical as a trading route. (Modern road-building has since made Fraser's route part of the Trans-Canadian Route, for today's roads and railroads can run beside the river, thus avoiding the rapids.)

The explorer who finally found a practical route across the mountains was named David Thompson. Ironically, Thompson was not even looking for a way west. He was exploring and surveying the Columbia River, from its source right on to the sea. In the process, he crossed Howse Pass, which became the main way to cross the Canadian Rockies. From Howse Pass, it was possible to reach the Columbia River system, which led on to the Pacific Ocean. Now there was a usable route west. But for many decades, the part of the Trans-Canada Route that was most commonly used went only as far as Lake Huron. That part of the route is still Canada's most heavily populated area.

## CHANGING TIMES

In the late 18th and in the 19th centuries, a number of changes occured that would transform the Trans-Canada Route.

***The American Revolution.*** First among these was the American Revolution. In 1776, the 13 British colonies below Canada declared their independence from Great Britain. They fought with the British and won. As a result, a dispute broke out over the territory west of the Great Lakes—was it part of the new United States or was it part of the British colony of Canada?

The disputed territory included the Pigeon River portion of La Vérendrye's westward route. This land finally became part of the United States when the dispute was resolved some 50 years later, in 1842. As a result, Canadians were forced north of the new boundary, which required them to use the older, more roundabout route north of Lake Superior.

In 1803, the United States further expanded its borders through the Louisiana Purchase. The French sold thousands of acres of land in the midwest and the Pacific northwest to the United States. Thus the southern portion of the Great Plains (what today are the U.S. states of North and South Dakota) was no longer Canadian land.

The Trans-Canada Route was dealt a further blow in 1821, when the two main fur companies—Hudson's Bay and the Northwest Company—merged into one and was called Hudson's Bay Company. After that, the main traffic of the fur trade began to head toward York Factory and Churchill, where the old Hudson's Bay Company used to have its headquarters. Thus the Trans-Canada fur trade route west of Montreal lost much of its importance.

***The Oregon–British Columbia Boundary.*** An important boundary dispute of the 1840s further affected the Trans-Canada Route. When the boundary between the U.S. state of Oregon and the Canadian territory of British Columbia was finally settled, the Canadians found themselves cut off from the rich Columbia River basin. They could no longer use this handy river system to reach the ocean. They then had to cut a passage through the lower Fraser River area in order to reach the Pacific.

***The Dominion of Canada.*** Until 1867, there had been many different parts of Canada—and all were subject to rule from Britain, just as the United States had been a century earlier. But in 1867 the various provinces of Canada *confederated*, or joined, to form a single nation, which was given *dominion*, or self-rule. Canada had become an independent nation (although the British government still had various decision-making rights over Canadian affairs).

Two years later, in 1869, the Hudson's Bay Company gave up the territorial rights it had held in northern and western Canada. Since Canada was now a self-governing nation, no company or organization could hold such power. Finally all parts of Canada were united under one government which was actually based within Canada. With that change, the settlement of western Canada really took hold. The fur traders were replaced by immigrants, looking for land and jobs as they moved west.

What did these changes mean for the Trans-Canada Route? As we have seen, they forced changes in the direction and course of the route, forcing it northward at Lake Superior, the Great Plains, and the Columbia River system. Also, because of the large flow of immigrants with their families to the west, an overland route following the same trail became necessary, rather than a simple canoe route.

Corduroy roads of logs, sometimes built out into balconies like this one, were the forerunners of the elaborate wooden trestles that would bear railroads westward. (From W. C. Bryant, *Picturesque America*, 1872)

## The Road West

Settlers in Canada, like those in the United States, traveled by wagon, not by canoe. As they traveled west across the plains, they created rough wagon roads wherever they could.

***The Canadian National Railway.*** In 1871, only four years after the Dominion of Canada was created, planning for the first trans-Canadian railroad began. As did railroads in the United States, this railroad went through several financial scandals and changes of route. Land becomes much more valuable to people if a railroad runs through it, as the railroad and its stations attract people and goods. Therefore many people bribed railroad officials and planners, trying to get the route to run near their land.

The railway ran into another kind of obstacle, as well. A man called Louis Riel led a revolt of Native Americans and of the *métis*, who were half-Indian and half-French. Riel and the métis wanted an independent, Catholic, French-oriented country of their own in the west. The Native Americans wanted protection from the railroad, which they thought would destroy their way of life by bringing in thousands of new settlers.

Riel and his rebels put up a good fight. Finally, though, the Canadian government put the revolt down and the railroad continued to be built. The last spike of the railroad was driven on November 7, 1885. From then on, the railroad was the main route west.

The new railway lines were directly across the plains, cutting through all natural obstacles in their path. When the railroad engineers came to the Rocky Mountains, they chose a route south of Howse Pass, going instead through Kicking Horse, Rogers, and Eagle passes. Remember that Howse Pass had been chosen because it led easily to the Columbia River system. Railroad builders did not need to be concerned with following a river. So the new technology of the railroad led to a new variation on an old route west.

This view of the modern railroad route shows the beauty and difficulty early travelers met in British Columbia. (Canadian Pacific Railroad)

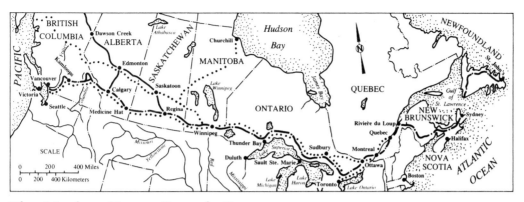

## The Modern Trans-Canada Routes

—·—·— Trans-Canada Highway  —··—··— U.S. - Canada Boundaries

————— Alaska Highway  ——————· State or Province Boundaries

·········· Main Railroad Routes

**A New Highway.** In 1962, the railroad was joined by a new kind of road—the 4,860-mile Trans-Canada Highway. This stretches all the way from St. John's, Newfoundland, to Victoria, British Columbia. From just inside the Gulf of St. Lawrence all the way to Vancouver, the highway runs roughly parallel to the old main Canadian route west, the same route initiated by Jacques Cartier in 1534 and completed by David Thompson in 1812. Many of the world's historic trade and travel routes are used no more, or are changed so much that it is hard to recognize them. But in modern-day Canada, the way west still follows the same course as it has done throughout history.

## SUGGESTIONS FOR FURTHER READING

Berton, Pierre. *The Impossible Railway* (New York: Knopf, 1972).

Brebner, John Bartlett. *The Discovery of North America, 1492-1806* (New York: Doubleday, 1955).

Burpee, Lawrence J. *An Historical Atlas of Canada* (Toronto: Nelson, 1927).

———. *The Search for the Western Sea*, two volumes (New York: Macmillan, 1936).

———. *The Discovery of Canada* (Toronto: Macmillan, 1944).

Creighton, Donald. *A History of Canada* (Boston: Houghton Mifflin, 1954).

Cumming, W. P. et al. *The Exploration of North America* (New York: Putnam, 1976).

De Voto, Bernard. *The Courage of Empire* (Boston: Houghton Mifflin, 1952).

Guillet, Edwin C. *The Story of Canadian Roads* (Toronto: University of Toronto Press, 1966).

Josephy, Alvin M. *The Indian Heritage of America* (New York: Knopf, 1969).

Lavendar, David. *Winner Take All* (New York: McGraw-Hill, 1977).

Munro, William Bennett. *Crusaders of New France* (New Haven: Yale University Press, 1918), volume 4 in the Chronicles of America Series.

Parkman, Francis. *France and England in North America* (London: Faber & Faber, 1954), edited by Samuel Eliot Morison.

———. *La Salle and the Discovery of the Great West* (Boston: Little, Brown, 1897).

Wrong, George M. *The Conquest of New France* (New Haven: Yale University Press, 1918), volume 10 in the Chronicles of America Series.

# 5

# THE NORTHEAST
# PASSAGE

The Northeast Passage is the world's most unlikely sea route. This most dangerous route links the Atlantic and Pacific oceans through Europe's Arctic Ocean—across the top of the world. That this route exists at all is due to the great European desire for Asian markets, to the powerful Russian drive toward the Pacific, and to modern technology. The route is so difficult that it has been open for regular use only since World War II.

The Northeast Passage follows a course for many thousands of miles above the Arctic Circle. It starts at the North Cape of the Scandinavian Peninsula. From there, it runs along the north coast of Siberian Asia, across several gulfs of the Arctic Ocean. Then this passage moves through the Bering Strait, which separates Asia and North America, and around the great peninsula of Kamchatka to the ports of the northern Pacific. It is a very dangerous route through a frozen world. Yet its importance to Russia's navy and to Russian development of Siberia's enormous resources has made it one of the most significant sea routes of the modern world.

People originally searched for the Northeast Passage because they wanted to find the way to the riches of the Far East. For many hundreds of years, Europeans had depended on Arab traders to bring them precious goods from China, Japan, India, and other Eastern lands. Spices, silks, cottons, jewels, and other finely made goods could only be obtained from the East—and for a long time, Europeans had no idea how to reach this fabled land.

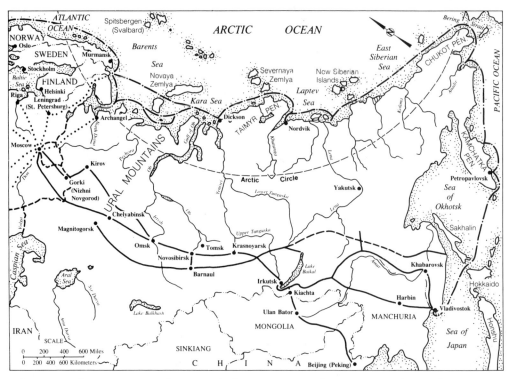

## The Northwest Passage and the Trans-Siberian Railroad

—·—·— Northeast Passage

———— Trans-Siberian Railroad

————·· Under Construction

············ Connecting Railroads

–––––– Main Canal-River Connections

This drive to the East was responsible for voyages like that of Christopher Columbus, who set off from Spain in 1492 trying to find a quick route to India. Ironically, the land he discovered instead—the continents of North and South America—proved in the long term to be far more profitable to Europeans than the quick route to the East that they were actually looking for.

However, it took Europeans a long time to realize how important the continents of North and South America could be to them. For years, explorers in North America searched for a Northwest Passage—a way to sail from the Atlantic to the Pacific via Canada's rivers and seas (see Chapter 3). Finally, the Europeans realized the enormous wealth that they had found in North America itself. And when they finally forged the Northwest Passage—a route that passed through the Arctic Ocean—it turned out to be almost unusable, since it passed through such cold and stormy seas.

In the same way, the search for a Northeast Passage through Siberia proved to be difficult. It took centuries before such a route was found, and even then, the route was very hard to use. But in the meantime, exploration of the eastern part of Russia opened up new and unexpected riches—the vast resources of Siberia.

## The Early Days of Russia

The push to explore the Northeast Passage did not originally come from the Russians. The early Russians were not innately a seagoing people. The country was founded in the ninth century by Swedish Vikings. The Vikings were pirates who sailed from Sweden, Norway, and Denmark to many parts of Europe, including England, France, and Iceland. The Norse or Norwegian Vikings went west, to Greenland and Newfoundland in North America. But the Swedish Vikings went east. The local inhabitants called these Swedes *Rus*, which is how the land came to be known as Russia.*

The local inhabitants of Russia were not Scandinavian; they were Slavs. Although they had little experience of ocean sailing, they were skilled at sailing on their country's many rivers. Even though the country of Russia was gradually expanding, the Russians did little to explore the Northeast Passage.

## The English

***The Age of Exploration.*** The English, on the other hand, were quite eager to explore new ocean routes of all kinds by the end of the 15th century. This was a very exciting period in Europe, which historians have called the *Renaissance*, or rebirth. This is because there was a general reawakening of interest in gaining knowledge and expanding the limits of existing ideas and knowledge. Scientists demanded that every theory in anatomy, physics, and astronomy be looked at, revised, and experimented with. Explorers became intent on proving the Ancient Greek theory that the world was round,

---

* *Russia* used to be the name of a smaller country that expanded as it conquered many other countries, becoming known in the process as the *Russian Empire*. In 1917, the Russians mounted a revolution to overthrow their rulers and form a new kind of government. They called their new country the *Union of Soviet Socialist Republics* or the *Soviet Union*. The Soviet Union consisted of many different kinds of people and nationalities, only one of which was the Russians. Nowadays, Russia itself is technically only one *republic*—a unit like a state, or a province—in the larger Soviet Union, though the Soviet Union is still often referred to simply as Russia.

instead of flat. Even artists were experimenting with new ways of drawing, and with reviving the old Greek ideas about using anatomy to show realistic portrayals of the human body.

One of the most important aspects of the Renaissance was the increase in new exploration activity. Much of this was motivated by the Europeans' desire to find their own route to the East. Although they had been receiving goods from the East for a long time, they had only vague ideas of where the countries of the East were, and how to reach them.

The Spanish financed Christopher Columbus's voyage to the west. That was supposed to open up new routes to the East, although it actually led to the European discovery of the West Indies. The Portuguese financed voyages to the south, which were responsible for charting out the Cape of Good Hope Route around the southern tip of Africa, and on to the rich lands of the East.

Meanwhile, the French were exploring the northern waters of the Atlantic. They sent many expeditions westward, to North America, hoping to find the Northwest Passage to China and India.

Where could the English find a place to break in? They were well equipped for trade and exploration. Their sailors had been in service in the navies of many other European governments as well as their own, so they had good sailing skills and the best knowledge at that time about geography and navigation. The English merchants had worked in cities like Seville, Spain's home base for the West Indies trade. They knew everything that was known at the time about foreign trade and new exploration.

But the English also had a disadvantage: most of the exploration routes had already been claimed by other European countries. The Portuguese controlled the Cape of Good Hope Route south around Africa. The Spanish held the Indies route west. The Turks had blocked Mediterranean and overland routes to the East. So the English decided to look to the north. The English Company of Merchant-Adventurers put the situation this way:

> ...there is left but one way to discover, which is into the North, for...
> of the four parts of the worlde, it seemeth three parts are discovered
> by other Princes.

***Northern Explorers.*** Some of the British voyages went to the northwest. Like the French, they searched for the Northwest Passage, through Canada to the Pacific Ocean. John Cabot, for example, led expeditions to Canada and in 1497 became the first European to touch the North American mainland (with the possible exception of the Vikings). But other British journeys went toward the northeast.

Some British explorers worked both ways. Sebastian Cabot, son of John Cabot, had searched for the Northwest Passage in 1509. In 1548, he was one of the men who formed the Company of Merchant-Adventurers, in order to fund an expedition to the northeast.

***Difficult Voyages.*** The English mounted several expeditions to the northeast, all of which faced great dangers, some of which did not come back.

The first voyage left in 1553 with a fleet of three ships. The ships were soon separated by storms off Norway, and one ship was lost. The *flagship*, or lead ship, crossed Arctic waters and entered the Kara Sea. In those northern waters, winter came early—in late August! Winter meant icy seas, which blocked the ship from further progress. So the crew turned back and set up winter quarters on the Russian mainland.

In his log entry for September 18, 1553, the captain, Sir Hugh Willoughby, describes the place they landed:

> …wherein were very many seal fishes [seals] and other great fishes, and…we saw bears, great deer, foxes, with divers [various] strange beasts…which to us were unknown, and also wonderful. Thus remaining in this haven the space of a week, and seeing the year far spent, and also very evil weather, as frost, snow, and hail, as though it had been the deep of winter, we thought it best to winter there. Wherefore we sent out three men south-southwest, to search if they could find people, who went three days' journey, but could find none. After that, we sent other three westward four days' journey, which also returned without finding any people. Then sent we three men southeast three days' journey, who in like sort returned without finding of people, or any similitude of habitation.

These are the last official words we have from Willoughby and his crew, except for a will dated January 1554. Before the spring came, everyone on his ship had died. Their frozen bodies and their log books were found by Russian fishermen the following year.

The third English ship on this first expedition had more luck. It entered the White Sea, which was more protected than the Kara. There it found a small fishing village, which in modern days has become the city of Archangel. The captain of that ship, Richard Chancellor, found that the natives were "amazed with the strange greatness of his ship (for in those parts before that time they had never seen the like)."

At first, these fishermen ran away from the strange English ship and its crew. But Chancellor ran after them and asked them questions. He soon found out that he had arrived at a country called Russia. The country was sometimes also known as *Muscovy* (or *Moscow*, which is the name of the capital city of Russia).

At this time, the ruler of Russia was known as a *tsar*, or emperor. When Chancellor learned where the tsar held his court, he arranged to be carried there by sled—even though it was almost 1,500 miles away, across snowy and deserted fields and forests. Chancellor wrote that he had to go by sled because:

> ...the people almost [do not know]...any other manner of carriage. The cause whereof is the exceeding hardness of the ground congealed in the wintertime by the force of the cold, which in those places is very extreme and horrible...

In Moscow, Chancellor was warmly welcomed. The tsar at this time was named Ivan, but later historians nicknamed him "Ivan the Terrible," for he had a reputation for being cruel. However, it was Ivan the Terrible who began Russian trade with England. When Chancellor returned home to England, he took with him the first Russian ambassador ever to appear at an English court, as well as good trade agreements.

Sebastian Cabot was well pleased with Chancellor's success and renamed his company the Muscovy Company. A regular trade was set up between London and Archangel. Archangel—which the Russians called Arkhangelsk—was ice-bound for four months of the year. Even so, it was Russia's major northern port for over a century.

During the next 30 years, some English sailors continued to search for the Northeast Passage. But none were able to pass from the White Sea into the Kara Sea. They were blocked by ice in the Kara Straits, the narrow waters on both sides of Vaigach Island.

Ice was not the only danger. Even though the Russians thought that the English had large ships, the ships were actually rather frail, and were small enough to be endangered by the whales that lived in this sea. Master Steven Burroughs, traveling west of the Kara Straits in 1556, relates a terrifying experience that his ship had with whales:

> On Saint James...day...there was a monstrous whale aboard of us [near us], so near to our side that we might have thrust a sword or any other weapon in him, which we durst [dared] not do for fear he

should have overthrown our ship. And then I called my company together, and all of us shouted, and with the cry that we made he departed from us...and at his falling down he made such a terrible noise in the water that a man would greatly have marveled, except he had known the cause of it. But God be thanked, we were quietly delivered of him.

In 1584, an English party did go through the Kara Straits and crossed the normally ice-clogged Kara Sea to the great Ob River. But from there they turned back. The English were not able to find a safe route through to the northeast and there their efforts rested.

## The Dutch

Another northern people, the Dutch, were also interested in northern trade. By 1577 they had joined the seagoing trade through the White Sea. Soon, Dutch ships came to outnumber the English ones.

***William Barents, Dutch Explorer.*** The Dutch also wanted to find the Northeast Passage, and they sent explorer William Barents on longer expeditions between 1594 and 1596. On his first voyage, Barents made it to the Ob River. But on his second voyage, the weather was so bad that the Kara Straits were packed with ice, barring the way completely.

On his third voyage, Barents changed his course. Instead of going northeast, he went straight north, across the sea that was later named the Barents Sea in his honor. In the process, he discovered Spitzbergen, a large island that was about as far north as northern Greenland. But Barents did not find the Northeast Passage and, although it was only August 26, the ice conditions were so bad that he was not even able to sail back home. As Barents described it:

> ...the ice began to drive with such force that we were enclosed round about therewith, and yet we sought all the means we could to get out, but it was all in vain...The same day in the evening, we got to the west side of the Ice Haven, where we were forced, in great cold, poverty, misery, and grief, to stay all that winter.

There they stayed, ferrying driftwood on rough sledges from four miles away to build their winter quarters. Their ships were slowly crushed by the ice, which Barents said was "most fearful both to see and hear, and made all the hair of our heads to rise upright with fear."

With tools like those lying on the ice, Barents's crewmen attempted to chop a passageway through the ice before the ship was caught fast. (Woodcut by De Veer, from *Relation des Trois Voyages des Bateaux Hollandais et Zelandais au Nord de la Norvège, Muscovie Russie et Tartarie*, 1598)

This group was luckier than Willoughby's men had been. Barents himself died, but most of the crew survived. After the spring thaw, they made a near-miraculous voyage back to the mainland in the small, open boats that they had salvaged from their ships.

***Giving Up.*** In the next few years, a few other explorations were made, including one by Henry Hudson. (Hudson is more famous for his discovery of Hudson's Bay in North America, where he died searching for a north*west* passage.) However, by the end of the 17th century, both the English and the Dutch had given up the idea of a north*east* passage, for they believed that the way would always be blocked by ice.

Meanwhile, trade continued with Archangel. But even that declined after 1620, when the Russian Tsar at that time cut foreign trade.

## THE COSSACKS

In the 17th century, a new kind of activity was seen on the eastern end of what would later become the Northeast Passage. The Cossacks began their eastward movement across Siberia toward the Pacific coast.

Barents and his crew faced danger not only from the ice and cold, but also from polar bears, who ruled the north country. (Woodcut by De Veer, from *Relation des Trois Voyages des Bateaux Hollandais et Zelandais au Nord de la Norvège, Muscovie Russie et Tartarie*, 1598)

The Cossacks were a mixed group of people who originally lived north of the Black and Caspian seas. Many of these people had been *serfs*, or peasant slaves, who had run away from their lords, seeking freedom. Their name comes from the Turkish word *kazak*, which means "adventurer" or "free person." The Cossacks were both, for though they had originally been runaway slaves, they became raiders who stole land from other people in the name of the Russian government.

The Cossacks spread throughout the vast land, following the network of great rivers that lace through Siberia. In that period, the prime resource of the region was furs—and the Cossacks took plenty of them. They followed the fur-bearing animals along the Siberian rivers, which flow north—rivers like the Ob, the Yenisey, the Lena, and the Kolima.

In that way, the Cossacks continued north to what they called the "Cold Ocean" (the Arctic) and east to the "Great Southern Ocean" (the Pacific). They also explored the Chukot Peninsula, which reaches across almost to touch North America. They also explored the Kamchatka Peninsula, which points down into the northern Pacific.

However, the Cossacks were not sailors. They used small boats to explore, but they did not set any course to steer by, for they did not have knowledge of the art of navigation. Nor did they know how to make maps of their journeys. One group even ended up on the North American coast, thinking it was just another island.

What the Cossacks did do was claim huge tracts of land for Russia. Before the Cossacks spread through Siberia, it had been populated by native peoples, much like those in Canada and the United States. These peoples had their own language, culture, and religion. The Cossacks, with their European weapons, were easily able to go where they wanted and to ignore the claims of the native peoples.

The Cossacks went down as far south as the Amur River, which even today is a border between the Soviet Union and China. They reached as far east as the Sea of Okhotsk, on the Pacific, and south of that, the Sea of Japan, also on the Pacific. They actually went *east* of Siberia, to the Pacific coast region that today is known as the "Soviet Far East."

## PETER THE GREAT

The Cossacks had claimed a vast territory with a huge coastline. This inspired the Russian tsar, Peter the First, also known as Peter

Even when the port was frozen, activity in Archangel proceeded on foot or on sleds pulled by reindeer. (By B. Peeters, National Maritime Museum)

the Great. Peter the Great was the first Russian tsar to take a great interest in the West and to study the knowledge of the rest of Europe. He had grand dreams for his country, which he wanted to make a great sea power. He also hoped to find the Northeast Passage.

Peter went to Archangel to study English and Dutch ships, so that he could provide his country with the latest knowledge of shipbuilding, sailing, and navigation. He also sent Russians to Western European ports to learn these skills. And he sent explorers to learn more about the far Pacific coast.

***Asia or America?*** At this time, there was one big question about world geography that still had not been answered. Were Asia and America separate continents? Or were the two land masses connected, even by a narrow strip of land?

Peter sent many Russian expeditions to find out—but each was unsuccessful. He then brought in outside experts, led by the Danish navigator Vitus Bering. Peter had Bering build several institutions on the Kamchatka Peninsula: a ship-building station, a naval academy, and an ironworking plant that could make anchors and other iron fittings for the ships. This was a much-needed improvement, for earlier Russian ships had been built completely of wood, and other Europeans had wondered how such fragile ships could stand the Arctic storms!

Bering also conducted an expedition for Peter. Using a mainly Western European crew, he sailed northeast from Kamchatka along the coast, through what is now called the Bering Strait, in his honor. Bering then went west, reaching the Kolima River on the Arctic Ocean. There he was blocked by ice. But although he could not go on, Bering had found that Asia and North America were, indeed, separate land masses, separated by the Bering Strait.

## OPENING THE PASSAGE

***Catherine the Great.*** Another important Russian ruler was Catherine the Great. She too expanded the borders of the Russian empire, and helped to sponsor the search for the Northeast Passage.

This passage was becoming more important all the time. Siberia was being traversed more frequently, especially by traders with China and trappers of valuable fur. Because this wild land had no roads, travelers went by river whenever they could. When they could

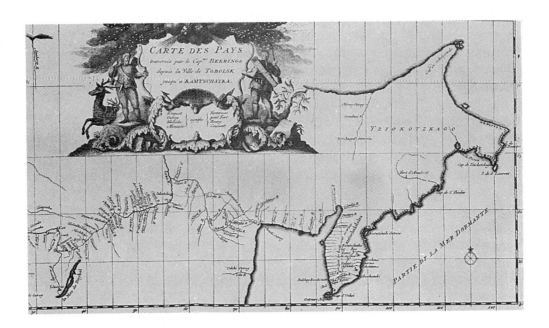

It was Vitus Bering who discovered, once and for all, that Asia and North America were not joined together, but were separated by a neck of water named, after him, the Bering Strait. (From J-B. B. d'-Anville, *Nouvel Atlas de la Chine*, Paris 1737)

not go by river, they had to *portage*, to carry their boats and their cargoes overland. As trade and trapping increased, it became more difficult and expensive to use this river-and-portage means of transportation. A northeast passage would mean that goods could be carried all the way by ship.

By the middle of the 18th century, under Catherine's rule, most of the Northeast Passage had been traveled and surveyed. People understood sections of this important route. But no one had yet traveled along the whole route. Ice from the Arctic Ocean still blocked this path for most of the year.

***Regular Trade.*** More was becoming known about the Northeast Passage route all the time. And ships were becoming larger, which meant that they were better able to stand the difficult voyage.

Gradually, merchant sailors developed regular trading routes out of Archangel, going first to the Ob River, then to the Yenisey. By the second half of the 19th century, ships from Western Europe had managed to travel hundreds of miles along these great rivers into the heart of Siberia. There they had traded for profitable cargo, such as grain and tallow (a kind of fat used to make candles and fuel for lamps). All of this laid the basis for the first continuous trip along the Northeast Passage.

Like many other major explorations along this route, the first complete trip was not made by a Russian. The Swedish Baron Nils Nordenskjöld set off on the first trip in 1878. This baron had earlier made several commercial trips to the Siberian rivers. During these trips he realized that these rivers brought warmer waters from the south to the Arctic Ocean. Therefore, the baron carefully timed his trip to take advantage of these warmer waters. The baron worked his way carefully along the coast from Sweden, until finally he entered the Kara Sea, where the British captain Willoughby and his crew had frozen to death so many years before.

**Meeting the Chukchi.** From the time he had entered the Kara Sea, Nordenskjöld had seen "neither men nor human habitations, if I except the old uninhabited hut between Cape Chelyuskin and the Khatanga River." So when the party saw two boats off Cape Shelagsky, on the Chukchi Peninsula, they were wild with excitement:

> Every man, with the exception of the cook, who could be induced by no catastrophe to leave his pots and pans and who had circumnavigated Asia and Europe perhaps without having been once on land, rushed on deck.

The Chukchi people that Nordenskjöld found were native people who spoke no Russian. However, one young boy could count to 10 in English! This showed that American whalers had probably been here before them. In any case, the two groups of people had to use sign language, for they had no common language.

**Trapped!** On September 28, 1878, Nordenskjöld stopped off shore at Kolyuchin Bay, near the top of the Chukchi Peninsula. In the morning, he found that the night's frost had firmly bound together all the ice that had been drifting in the water. Now his ship could not move.

At first, Nordenskjöld wasn't worried, for he knew that many American whalers had stayed in this area until as late as the middle of October. After all, he thought, it would only take "a few hours' southerly wind sufficient to break up the belt of ice." The ice was hardly wider than a Swedish mile, or less than seven English miles.

But gradually, the baron realized that the warm wind would not be coming. He would have to spend the winter north of the Arctic Circle.

Luckily for him and his crew, the baron had the benefit of earlier experience. The ship was not in danger of being crushed (although he had stored some vital items on shore, just in case). The crew actually survived very well on board, without even any serious cases of frostbite:

> On board vessel in our cabins and collection rooms it was...by no means so cold as many would suppose...Much greater inconvenience than from cold did we in the cabins suffer from the excessive heat and the fumes which firing in large cast-iron stoves is wont to cause in small close rooms.

However, we can imagine how frustrated the baron probably was when he realized that if he had moved his ship even a few hours earlier, he probably would not have had to spend the winter in that way! In fact, his ship did not get free until July 18th of the following year.

***The Journey Completed.*** And by 11 A.M. on July 19th, the journey was complete:

> ...we were in the middle of the sound which united the North Polar Sea [the Arctic Ocean] with the Pacific, and from this point the *Vega* [the baron's ship] greeted the Old and New worlds by a display of flags and firing of a Swedish salute...Now for the first time, after the lapse of three hundred and twenty-six years, and when most men experienced in sea matters had declared the undertaking impossible, was the Northeast Passage at last achieved.

Nordenskjöld was rightly proud of his achievement, which he had accomplished "without the sacrifice of a single human life." However, he was far too hopeful about the future of the route. He believed that "the same thing may be done again in most, perhaps in all, years in the course of a few weeks." In fact, there were still many dangers on this icy route. The next person who tried the Northeast Passage, in 1900, died in the attempt. Nevertheless, the Russian government persisted in trying to develop this useful route.

***New Activity in Siberia.*** Other governments were also eager for the Siberian trade. In 1896, the Russian government gave special

terms to an English company for setting up trade on the west Siberian rivers. By 1905, a fleet of 22 ships was sailing in the Yenisey River. When the western port of St. Petersburg, on the Baltic Sea, had become an important trading center, Archangel had declined in importance. Now it began to revive as a major northern port.

Sea trade also developed at the other end of the route. The Russians built a prime port, Vladivostok, on the Sea of Japan. Although this city was ice-bound for three months of the year, during the warmer months it became the home port of a fleet of steamships that sailed through the Bering Strait to the Kolima River.

Baron Nordenskjöld's sailing ship *Vega*, accompanied by the *Lena*, celebrates her arrival off the northernmost point in Asia, Cape Chelyuskin, in 1879.
(Anonymous engraving from M. Kiold, *The Voyage of the Vega*)

## INTO THE ARCTIC

***Technical Advances.***   In addition to exploring their Siberian territories, the Russians also explored their portion of the Arctic. Their expeditions were much helped by the technical advances of the late 19th and early 20th centuries. One important technical advance was the development of much more accurate surveying equipment.

A century after Vitus Bering had established a shipbuilding center there, Petropavlovsk on Kamchatka Peninsula was still a very quiet port. (Lithograph by Kittlibt, from *Voyage of Lutke*, 1826-9)

Surveying equipment is used to process information so that accurate maps can be made, showing the correct distances between different points, the correct locations of rivers and mountains, etc. Another aid to exploration was the wireless radio, which allowed an explorer to maintain communication with others even when a ship was far out at sea.

Perhaps the most important technical improvement was the specially reinforced ship known as an *icebreaker*. These icebreakers were mostly converted whaling ships, all foreign-built, usually by the British.

With this equipment, the Russians moved to explore fully the islands they had claimed in the Arctic Ocean. Some of these islands had in fact been discovered by the British, American, or Canadian explorers, but Russia moved to press its claim to them.

***Russians in North America.*** During the height of their exploration, the Russians had fur trading outposts along the west coast of North America, reaching as far south as Fort Ross, just north of San Francisco. This was land that the Cossacks or explorers like Bering had claimed.

By the end of the 19th century, the Russians had long since abandoned most of these settlements, for they had become part of the United States and Canada. Alaska, which the Russians had once owned, had been sold to the United States in 1867.

By this time, the Russians were more eager than ever to develop the Northeast Passage—but they were no longer interested in it for the China trade. Rather, they wanted it to protect and develop their land.

Such a route became even more important when war threatened, as was frequently the case at the turn of the century. War could cut off Russia from Europe's large inland seas—the Baltic, the Black, and the Mediterranean. In wartime, Russian ships going from Europe to East Asia might be forced to take a long and roundabout trip through the Suez Canal, around Africa, or (after it was built) through the Panama Canal. The Northeast Passage—which the Russians called the "Northern Sea Route"—would mean that the Russians could still transport goods via a shorter route. The Northeast Passage had shown its usefulness in the 1890s, when metal for the new Trans-Siberian Railway had been shipped across the Arctic and inland along the Yenisey River.

***Europe and the Northeast Passage.*** Norway was also interested in the route. In 1912, the Norwegians established a steamship company to operate between their capital, Oslo, and the Yenisey River.

The route became useful to the rest of Europe during World War I, when most of the countries of Europe were at war with one another. The countries that were fighting with Russia, known as the Allies, were anxious to receive food supplies from Siberia. A good deal of food came from the Yenisey wheatlands, along the Northern Sea Route. This route was secure from the fighting, because it was so far north. To make the food transportation even more certain, Britain built four icebreakers for Russia and sent five others from Canada.

## THE RUSSIAN REVOLUTION

Then, in 1917, the Russian people overthrew their rulers, the tsars, in an event known as the Russian Revolution. Eventually, the people who were behind the revolution set up a new system of government, known as socialism. They called their new country the Union of Soviet Socialist Republics, or the Soviet Union.

***The Soviet Civil War.*** Many people in the Soviet Union supported the tsar and his rule, or at least did not believe in the new form of government. They fought against the new revolutionary government, in the Soviet Civil War. Many countries in Europe also did not like the Russians' new system of socialist government. They joined in the Civil War on the side that was against the socialists.

The Allies—the countries that had fought with Russia during World War I—sent troops to help fight against the socialists. The British were especially close to the tsar and his family, and they sent troops to fight in Russia, including men who landed at both Archangel and Murmansk (a small settlement east of the North Cape). These troops penetrated some distance inside Russia, but finally had to give up and leave. The United States also sent troops to this area.

When the Allied troops left and the Civil War was over, the new government faced many problems. The combination of trying to fight the Germans in World War I and then fighting the Allies and its own people in the Civil War had left the Soviet Union devastated. In Siberia, as everywhere else, food supplies were very short, especially in Archangel. To ease the famine, supplies of grain were brought in from northern Siberia through the Kara Sea, in a series of shipments over several years.

During this period, development of the Northeast Passage slowed, but did not stop completely. Two full trips from Vladivostok to Archangel were made. One was before the Revolution, in 1914, by a Russian named Boris Vilkitski. The other was after the Revolution, in 1918, made by the Norwegian explorer Roald Amundsen. (Amundsen was also the first person to complete the Northwest Passage between the Atlantic and Pacific oceans of North America, which he also made via the Arctic Ocean.) Both Amundsen and Vilkitski had to take two seasons to make their journeys, setting up camp for one winter on the way.

## More Technical Advances

Meanwhile, technical advances began to make the route more manageable. Navigators needed information on temperature and ice conditions, for they had only a two- to three-month season of fairly open water on the hardest parts of the route. Weather stations were set up around the Arctic. Only five were in place before the Revolution, but almost 70 more were set up in the next 20 years, including one at the North Pole.

Airplanes and helicopters were also brought in to help shipping. These vehicles could fly ahead of a ship to scout the best route through the floating ice. They could provide supplies for the distant weather stations around the Arctic. They could also perform rescue missions. That meant that scientists could set up temporary stations on ice floes, drifting with the ice, to chart a current's speed and direction. Then, when the ice became too small for safety, the scientists could signal a plane to pick them up and take them to a ship.

***Progress in the Arctic.*** These advances worked. In 1932, a ship made the first trip through the Northeast Passage in a single season. Even this trip was so hard that the ice broke every blade on the ship's propeller. To replace the blades, the crew had to shift hundreds of tons of coal into the bow (the front part of the ship) to raise the stern (the back part of the ship, where the propellers are). Then, when the propeller itself was lost, the ship had to use sails to pass through the Bering Strait. This was especially dangerous, for the ice was due to close only days later. The crew must have been very relieved when the trip was accomplished in time!

The success of this ship did not make the trip easier for other ships, however. The following year scientists tried to make the same trip in a more heavily reinforced ship, but they were locked in an ice field when winter came early. The ship then drifted toward Alaska, then further north, and finally sank. Thanks to modern technology, however, the crew was rescued, for they were able to radio for a plane to come in on a landing strip they had built on the ice.

## ICEBREAKERS

Clearly, if the Northeast Passage was to become a practical route between the east and the west coasts, heavier icebreakers were needed. One Soviet official put it this way:

> The aeroplane is the eye; the radio station is the ear; and the icebreaker is the fist in this work of ours.

The few icebreakers in use in the mid-1930s were old and makeshift, left over from those that the British had provided before the Revolution. But in 1932, the Soviets established a special

Northern Sea Route Administration to develop shipping along the route, and they began to build their own icebreakers.

In 1937, the first Soviet icebreakers were completed. These were larger and heavier than the old British ships. The old ships rammed into the ice, but the modern ships were designed to climb onto the edge of the ice and crush it. Some were built with tanks to take on extra water for more weight, and with heavy-duty engines to help the ship push the broken ice aside.

Progress varied. After a successful shipping season in 1936, 1937 saw some 26 ships stranded in the ice as winter closed in early. They were rescued—but the leaders of the Northern Sea Route Administration were fired for their failure! Only in 1939 did the Russians come to have what they saw as their first "normal" year along the Northeast Passage. Port Dickson, an Arctic shipping point, had a population of 3,000–4,000 during the shipping season, and was called one of the "liveliest points in the Arctic."

## WORLD WAR II

The Soviets made other changes that improved the route by linking it with inland waterways to western Russia. They built the White Sea Canal, which linked the Baltic and the White seas. For the first time, Russian ships could sail from the Baltic to the Pacific without passing through waters controlled by other countries.

Other inland waterways linked the Black and the Caspian seas. The canal and river system meant that the Soviets could much more easily ship goods within their huge country.

But they only had a short time to take full advantage of their expanded shipping network. In 1941 they were attacked by Nazi Germany and were drawn into World War II on the side of the Allies—Britain, France, and later, the United States. Murmansk was cut off and Finnish soldiers destroyed the White Sea Canal. Siberia once again supplied the White Sea region with food, fuel, and other vital resources.

The Germans were fully aware of the importance of the Northern Sea Route, which enabled the Soviets at least to move supplies and soldiers within their own country. In fact, the Germans attacked and took over Norway partly to be able to block this key Soviet route. At this time, their main focus of attack was the Soviet Union, and they wanted to make sure that English and American aid could not reach that country. Germany sent ships, airplanes, and submarines to attack Allied supply ships at the Atlantic entrance to the Northeast Passage.

***Anglo-American Aid.*** But English and American convoys continued to supply Russia's White Sea ports. They sent 739 ships in 3½ years, with 9 out of 10 reaching port safely.

Most of these sailors had never taken such icy voyages. They constantly had to remove the ice that would form on the exposed decks, so that the ships would not become topheavy. Submarine crews had to continually grease the hatch with gelatin so that the vessel could dive under water at a moment's notice to remove ice. Many of these sailors were later awarded medals by the Soviet government.

On the eastern end of the Northeast Passage, ships brought supplies from North American ports, like Seattle, into Russian ports between the Bering Strait and the Taimir Peninsula. These ships were less at risk, for the Siberian Sea was strange territory to enemy ships. As one World War II Soviet captain put it:

> You see, the ice is our friend. We can hide in the ice, if nothing else. There isn't a [German] warship commander who would dare follow us in.

In the middle section of the Northern Sea Route, Soviet ships continued to go back and forth, ferrying supplies. They were vital to the war effort—and they were also building up experience for the route that would be developed after the war.

## THE MODERN ROUTE

After World War II, the Soviet Union was once again devastated. Even after the war was over, the country still had few icebreakers, and some of them had to be returned to the United States a few years later. The ships they did have often had heavy fuel needs; they often had to make detours at special refueling stations along the way, losing valuable time.

But in the years after World War II, coal-burning icebreakers were largely replaced by oil-fueled ships, and even by some atomic-powered ones.

Sometimes only one icebreaker is sufficient to make the journey; sometimes they travel in groups. Either way, they now make it possible to double the time that the complete route is open, so that

Modern travelers wintering in the Arctic carry portable shelters and can be rescued by air, unlike Barents' crew, pictured here in their winter quarters. (Woodcut by De Veer, from *Relation des Trois Voyages des Bateaux Hollandais et Zelandais au Nord de la Norvège, Muscovie Russie et Tartarie*, 1598)

now it is possible to use the route for four months of the year or more. This gives much more flexibility to the hundreds of Soviet ships operating in the north.

The route is still a hard one for the sailors who travel on it. But the rewards are great, especially since the Soviets did manage to rebuild their inland waterways after World War II. Now they can move their ships from ocean to ocean, sea to sea, without interference from any other country.

Even when interference is not a problem, the saving in distance traveled is huge. Before the Northeast Passage was open, ships traveling between Murmansk and Vladivostok often went through the Panama Canal or around the Cape of Good Hope, both a distance of about 14,000 miles. But the Northern Sea Route between the two is only 6,000 miles.

How important the Northeast Passage will be in the future depends partly on the climate. For much of the 20th century, the Arctic has been warmer than in earlier centuries. Even if it does become yet warmer, however, technology may keep the route open.

In any case, the route greatly benefits the Soviet Union: the Soviets are thus able to continue to develop the rich Siberian lands that the Russians explored while seeking the Northeast Passage. Siberia is now an important source of oil, natural gas, and important minerals, as well as an agricultural area. Those who dreamed of the easy route through mild waters to the riches of the east would have been surprised by the riches that lay hidden in the frozen land of Siberia.

## Suggestions for Further Reading

Armstrong, Terence E. *The Northern Sea Route: Soviet Exploitation of the North East Passage* (Cambridge: Cambridge University Press, 1952).

Krypton, Constantine. *The Northern Sea Route and the Economy of the Soviet North* (New York: Praeger, 1956).

Mitchell, Mairin. *The Maritime History of Russia, 848-1948* (London: Sidgwick and Jackson, 1949; New York: Macmillan, 1949).

Penrose, Boies. *Travel and Discovery in the Renaissance, 1420-1620* (New York: Atheneum, 1975; reprint of the 1952 Harvard University edition).

Stefansson, Vilhjalmur, ed. *Great Adventures and Explorations: From the Earliest Times to the Present as Told by the Explorers Themselves*, revised edition (New York: Dial Press, 1952).

Tavernier, Bruno. *Great Maritime Routes: An Illustrated History* (New York: Viking, 1972), translated from the French.

# INDEX